ST. HUGO OF CENTRAL PARK

A PLAY

By
JEFFREY KINDLEY

SAMUEL FRENCH, INC.
45 West 25th Street   NEW YORK 10010
7623 Sunset Boulevard HOLLYWOOD 90046
LONDON   TORONTO

Dialogue Copyright ©, 1978, 1989, by Jeffrey Kindley
Lyrics Copyright ©, 1978, 1988, by Jeffrey Kindley

ALL RIGHTS RESERVED

CAUTION: *Professionals and amateurs are hereby warned that ST. HUGO OF CENTRAL PARK is subject to a royalty. It is fully protected under the copyright laws of the United States of America, the British Commonwealth, including Canada, and all other countries of the Copyright Union. All rights, including professional, amateur, motion pictures, recitation, lecturing, public reading, radio broadcasting, television, and the rights of translation into foreign languages are strictly reserved. In its present form the play is dedicated to the reading public only.*

ST. HUGO OF CENTRAL PARK *may be given stage presentation by amateurs in theatres seating less than 500 upon payment of a royalty of Fifty Dollars for the first performance, and Forty Dollars for each additional performance.* PLEASE NOTE: *for amateur productions in theatres seating over 500, write for special royalty quotation, giving details as to ticket price, number of performances and exact number of seats in your theatre. Royalties are payable one week before the opening performance of the play, to Samuel French, Inc., at 45 W. 25th St., New York, NY 10010; or at 7623 Sunset Blvd., Hollywood, CA 90046, or to Samuel French (Canada), Ltd., 80 Richmond St. East, Toronto, Ontario, Canada M5C 1P1.*

Royalty of the required amount must be paid whether the play is presented for charity or gain and whether or not admission is charged.

Stock royalty quoted on application to Samuel French, Inc.

For all other rights than those stipulated above, apply to Gilbert Parker at William Morris Agency, Inc., 1350 Ave. of the Americas, New York, NY 10019.

Particular emphasis is laid on the question of amateur or professional readings, permission and terms for which must be secured in writing from Samuel French, Inc.

Copying from this book in whole or in part is strictly forbidden by law, and the right of performance is not transferable.

Whenever the play is produced the following notice must appear on all programs, printing and advertising for the play: "Produced by special arrangement with Samuel French, Inc."

Due authorship credit must be given on all programs, printing and advertising for the play.

Anyone presenting the play shall not commit or authorize any act or omission by which the copyright of the play or the right to copyright same may be impaired.

No changes shall be made in the play for the purpose of your production unless authorized in writing.

The publication of this play does not imply that it is necessarily available for performance by amateurs or professionals. Amateurs and professionals considering a production are strongly advised in their own interests to apply to Samuel French, Inc., for consent before starting rehearsals, advertising, or booking a theatre or hall.

No part of this book may be reproduced, stored in a retrieval system, or transmitted in any form, by any means, including mechanical, electronic, photocopying, recording, or otherwise, without the prior written permission of the publisher.

ISBN 0 573 66016 6   Printed in U.S.A.

IMPORTANT BILLING AND CREDIT REQUIREMENTS

All producers of ST. HUGO OF CENTRAL PARK *must* give credit to the Author of the Play in all programs distributed in connection with performances of the Play and in all instances in which the title of the Play appears for purposes of advertising, publicizing or otherwise exploiting the Play and/or a production. The name of the Author *must* also appear on a separate line, in which no other name appears, immediately following the title, and *must* appear in size of type not less than fifty percent the size of the title type.

SAMUEL FRENCH, INC. can supply a piano/vocal score of the music to amateurs for a period of eight weeks upon receipt of the following:

1. Number of performances and exact performance dates.
2. $50.00 deposit, refundable immediately following the close of production, upon receipt of the material in good condition.
3. $25.00 blanket rental fee for entire run.
4. $3.00 postage and handling.

PLEASE NOTE: rental fee is not refundable in any event.

Stock terms quoted upon application.

Cover art by Bob Perkins. Used by permission, All Rights Reserved.

THE LAMB'S THEATRE COMPANY, LTD.

Carolyn Rossi Copeland
Producing Director

Joel K. Ruark
General Manager

presents

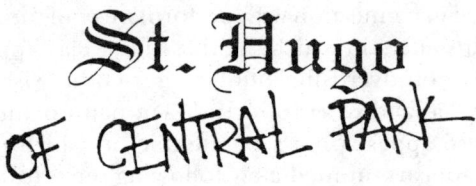
St. Hugo of Central Park

a new play by
Jeffrey Kindley

Directed by Robert Bridges

with

MACE BARRETT
MARILYN CASKEY
ROGER CHAPMAN
JEFF GARRETT

JAMES HARTMAN
ANNA HOLBROOK
IAN D. SHUPECK
JUDITH TILLMAN

Music by, Randy Courts
Set Design. Carl Baldasso
Costume Design. Barbara A. Bell
Lighting Design, Rachel Budin
Sound Design, Ed Fitzgerald
Production Stage Manager, Allison Rabenau
Technical Director, Paul Grigoridis

CAST

JEFF GARRETT	Hugo DePew
JUDITH TILLMAN	Emily DePew
MACE BARRETT	Edgar DePew, Hawker
ROGER CHAPMAN	Mr. Muncy, Elroy, Reporter, Mr. Pinckney, Ron Blodgett
MARILYN CASKEY	Dr. Kitchener, Judy, Reporter, Nurse Noble
ANNA HOLBROOK	Susie, Martha, Jill Gerard
IAN D. SHUPECK	John, Reporter, Dr. Petricoff
JAMES HARTMAN	Policeman, Reporter, Harley Goodrich, Perry Porter

THE PLAY TAKES PLACE IN NEW YORK CITY, 1959 TO 1968.

There will be a 10 minute intermission.

CHARACTERS

HUGO DEPEW
EMILY DEPEW, his mother
MR. MUNCY, a psychologist
SOLOIST
CHOIR
DR. KITCHENER, a psychiatrist
EDGAR DEPEW, Hugo's father
SUSIE, a hooker
MARTHA, an Eastsider
JOHN, her husband
JUDY, an aide at the Institute for the Blind
ELROY, a young blind man
POLICEMAN
REPORTER #1
REPORTER #2
REPORTER #3
REPORTER #4
DR. PETRICOFF, a medical researcher
NURSE NOBLE
MR. PINCKNEY, an elderly blind man
HARLEY GOODRICH, a TV evangelist
PERRY PORTER, a doll manufacturer
JILL GERARD, a TV gossip reporter
RON BLODGETT, a TV newsman
HAWKER
CHEERLEADERS

ST. HUGO OF CENTRAL PARK

ACT I
SCENE 1

AT RISE: Darkness. A sound of ticking. A SPOTLIGHT picks out HUGO DEPEW, a skinny young man inserting a clockwork mechanism into a hollowed-out cantaloupe. Although his age varies during the play from 17 to 26, he appears to be in his mid-twenties throughout.

A CHOIR enters and sings.

SOLOIST.
SAINT HUGO WAS A MARTYR;
HE DIED FOR YOU AND ME.
HIS LIFE WAS BRIEF BUT BEAUTIFUL.
HIS DEATH WAS ON TV.
CHOIR.
SAINT HUGO, OH, SAINT HUGO,
WHY WILL WE NEVER LEARN?
SAINTS ARE BORN TO LEAD THE WAY
AND NEVER TO RETURN.

(The CHOIR Exits and the LIGHTS fade on HUGO, coming up on a psychologist's office at the Wrigley Reformatory for Boys in Brooklyn. The year is 1959. MRS. DEPEW is speaking to MR. MUNCY, a psychologist.)

MRS. DEPEW. I hope you understand why my Hugo isn't like the others—I mean the other boys here at the reformatory.

MR. MUNCY. I do indeed. However, it would help in preparing his psychological profile if you could answer a few...

MRS. DEPEW. His father said to me this morning, tell Mr. Muncy that Hugo never stole anything that he couldn't have paid for out of his own allowance.

MR. MUNCY. I understand that, Mrs. DePew.

MRS. DEPEW. And the bomb threats—do you understand about the bomb threats? I wouldn't have thought anyone really cared about a teenage prank like that.

MR. MUNCY. Six of the bombs *did* go off.

MRS. DEPEW. That was an accident. When you plant 75 bombs around the city, it stands to reason that a few of them are going to go off accidentally. Hugo failed chemistry, you know.

MR. MUNCY. I know.

MRS. DEPEW. And when you say they went off—well, that isn't quite accurate, is it? I mean, when a bomb goes off it usually explodes. Hugo's bombs leaked. And did they injure anyone? No, they didn't. All this talk about the Mad Bomber of Brooklyn Heights just strikes me as ridiculous. And Father O'Flaherty got what he deserved. Anyone who holds a honeydew melon to his ear because he can hear it ticking...! We paid his drycleaning bill; what more does he want?

MR. MUNCY. Mrs. DePew...

MRS. DEPEW. Do you know how much they charge to clean a cassock nowadays?

MR. MUNCY. You're missing the point, I'm afraid. Why did Hugo plant 75 honeydew melons in 75 Catholic churches throughout the greater New York area? Why did he then call those churches and tell them that a large piece of fruit was about to go off unless they cancelled their Sunday services?

MRS. DEPEW. All right, all right. So he stole the melons.

MR. MUNCY. That wasn't my question, Mrs. DePew. Let me ask you this: Hugo was raised in the Catholic faith, was he not?

MRS. DEPEW. Yes.

MR. MUNCY. And he was an altar boy?

MRS. DEPEW. Yes, he was.

MR. MUNCY. When did he first begin to express doubts about the church?

MRS. DEPEW. Doubts? What kind of doubts?

MR. MUNCY. That's what I'm asking you.

MRS. DEPEW. I mean, what would he doubt? We went to church every Sunday for the past 17 years.

MR. MUNCY. And did he believe in the Catholic religion?

MRS. DEPEW. Hugo never missed a Sunday, not from the time he was two years old up until two months ago.

MR. MUNCY. He was a very religious boy, then.

MRS. DEPEW. Not at all. He's always been quite normal, Mr. Muncy. I can see what you're getting at, but believe me, there's never been anything in the least bit freaky about Hugo.

MR. MUNCY. But I just wanted to...

Mrs. Depew. He *hated* being an altar boy. His father and I always admired him for that, though of course we'd never tell him so.

Mr. Muncy. What?

Mrs. Depew. He wasn't like little Kevin what's-his-name. His parents used to talk about how he'd give Extreme Unction to his stuffed animals. Now, *there* was a child who'd really interest you—you being a psychologist, I mean.

Mr. Muncy. Right now I'm interested in Hugo. Did he ever explain to you or your husband why he felt compelled to make these threats?

Mrs. Depew. No.

Mr. Muncy. Did you ever ask?

Mrs. Depew. Edgar—my husband—asked him why honeydews.

Mr. Muncy. And?

Mrs. Depew. Hugo wouldn't say. Edgar was all upset because, as you probably know, he's *in* fruit, and he couldn't figure out why any child of his would have to steal somebody else's melons. What he suspected was that somehow he'd failed Hugo, because honeydews were one item he didn't stock in any quantity. So Edgar was in tears, saying, "Haven't I always given you everything you ever wanted?" and Hugo wouldn't say a word. I said to him, "Why didn't you tell us you needed some melons to make a few bombs?"—because of course we would have helped him out. We always have. But no, Hugo wouldn't say a word. Doesn't he talk to you, either?

Mr. Muncy. I've only met with your son twice, Mrs.

DePew, and both times he failed to communicate. I was hoping that today, with you and your husband present...

MRS. DEPEW. Edgar *wanted* to come, he really did.

MR. MUNCY. I was hoping that Hugo might open up a little.

(An object is hurled into the office and lands on the floor.)

MRS. DEPEW. What in the...! Mr. Muncy, what *is* that?

MR. MUNCY. It looks like a... Oh my God, it's a cantaloupe!

MRS. DEPEW. *(calling off)* Hugo! It's me! It's your mother! Hugo!

(The LIGHTS go down on the office and come up on HUGO, speaking to the audience.)

HUGO. I knew it was my mother. I thought my father would be there, too, but I wasn't surprised to find out that he couldn't make it. My father was one of those people who spend their lives trying to pretend that everything's okay, and since sooner or later everybody comes up against something that's *not* okay, he'd produced a very convenient ulcer that kept him from facing up to anything disagreeable. When I was in the Wrigley Reformatory for Boys he used to send me postcards every few weeks asking me how I was enjoying myself. At first I thought it was a joke, so I sent him a card that said "Having wonderful time, wish you were here," and the next thing I know he's asking me if I've earned any new merit badges. I really believe my father was convinced I spent two years of my life in a Boy Scout Camp. Anyway, on this particular day...

(There is a loud EXPLOSION from the direction of the now dark psychologist's office.)

HUGO. ...on this particular day when I threw the cantaloupe into Mr. Muncy's office, I was convinced that I was going to get three at one blow. As it turned out, I didn't get any of them—unless you count Mr. Muncy, who got part of the cantaloupe stuck in his ear. But you'll notice that this one did explode, which was some kind of victory in a way, and was due entirely to the education I got from some of my fellow J.D.'s at Wrigley. Now, the thing everybody wanted to know at the time, and the thing you probably wanna know right now, is: Why did I do it?

Well, I can tell you in a word: publicity. Probably you're thinking I was crazy or something, putting all these leaky honeydews in churches all over town and then using them as a threat. The first question I was asked when I got to Wrigley—this kid comes up to me and he says, "Didn't anybody ever teach you how to make a decent fire bomb?" But you see, that wasn't the point. I didn't want to start a fire; I didn't want to hurt anyone; I just wanted to get a little publicity and start people thinking. I had this terrific statement all written out for the newspapers, but my father's lawyer tore it up into little bits. He said it was better to spend two years in a reforma-

ACT I   ST. HUGO OF CENTRAL PARK   13

tory than the rest of my life in the State Hospital for the Criminally Insane. What it said was, "Beware of practicing your piety before men in order to be seen by them; for then you will have no reward from your Father who is in heaven." It sort of surprised me that people would think that was criminally insane, since I got it out of the Gospel according to St. Matthew and it was a direct quote from Jesus Christ. But then, I was in for a lot of surprises at the time. Where I went too far was in Mr. Muncy's office, because although Christ said that He had come to set the children against their parents, He didn't actually say that it was a good idea to try to blow them to bits with a cantaloupe.

(The LIGHTS go down on HUGO and come up on MR. MUNCY'S office again. MRS. DEPEW and MR. MUNCY are covered with the remains of the cantaloupe.)

   Mrs. Depew. Are you all right?
   Mr. Muncy. What?
   Mrs. Depew. I said, are you all right?
   Mr. Muncy. Why are you talking in that funny little faraway voice?
   Mrs. Depew. I'm not. This is the way I talk.
   Mr. Muncy. It wasn't the way you talked a minute ago. You sound like you're under water.
   Mrs. Depew. Well, I'm not. Pull yourself together, Mr. Muncy.
   Mr. Muncy. What?
   Mrs. Depew. *(louder)* Why would he do a thing like this to his own mother?

MR. MUNCY. Oedipal aggression.
MRS. DEPEW. What?
MR. MUNCY. Since he couldn't sleep with you...
MRS. DEPEW. What!
MR. MUNCY. *(after a beat)* I just realized my voice has changed, too.
MRS. DEPEW. It has not. Since he couldn't do *what?*
MR. MUNCY. Fornicate, Mrs. DePew. It's symbolic ejaculation.
MRS. DEPEW. Don't be ridiculous! Honestly, Mr. Muncy! He's my son! I love him! Oh Lord God in Heaven, why would he *do* this to me?

END OF SCENE 1

SCENE 2

A CHOIR appears and sings:

SOLOIST.
SAINT HUGO PLANTED MELONS
TO REAP THE SOULS OF MEN.
THEY TOOK AWAY HIS HONEYDEWS
AND PUT HIM IN THE PEN.
CHOIR.
SAINT HUGO, OH, SAINT HUGO,
WHY WILL WE NEVER LEARN?
SAINTS ARE BORN TO LEAD THE WAY

AND NEVER TO RETURN.
SAINT HUGO PLANTED MELONS
TO REAP THE SOULS OF MEN.
OF MEN.

(Crossfade on CHOIR as the LIGHTS come up on HUGO.)

HUGO. I learned many things at the Wrigley Reformatory, but the thing I wanted most to learn always seemed to escape me. Ever since I could remember, I wanted to be truly good. It's kind of hard to explain what I mean by that; it was just kind of a feeling I had. I guess a lot of you probably feel the same way. Now, in *my* family, wanting to be good wasn't a thing I could talk about or even admit to; and because most of the time when I was growing up I was actually just as rotten as the next kid, it never occurred to anybody that I had this great secret yearning to be good. Anyway, during my two years at Wrigley I had a lot of time to think. And one thing I learned was that psychoanalysis wasn't going to be any help at all.

(HUGO Enters the psychologist's office and the LIGHTS come up to reveal MR. MUNCY and DR. KITCHENER, a female psychiatrist. The year is 1961.)

MR. MUNCY. Dr. Kitchener, this is Hugo DePew. Hugo, Dr. Kitchener is a psychiatrist, and she's here to help you make the difficult transition back to Real Life.
DR. KITCHENER. How are you, Hugo?

HUGO. All right.

DR. KITCHENER. Well, I'm sure you *are* all right, too. I'm all right, and you're all right. The two of us are going to get along just fine. Mr. Muncy, Hugo and I want to have a little talk. Would you mind...?

MR. MUNCY. Could I have a word with you?

DR. KITCHENER. A word?

MR. MUNCY. In private.

DR. KITCHENER. Well, I don't see why you couldn't have a word with me in front of Hugo. We're all all right, you know.

MR. MUNCY. Two of us are all right.

DR. KITCHENER. Really? Which two?

MR. MUNCY. Doctor, I don't think you understand what I was telling you earlier...

DR. KITCHENER. That will be all, Mr. Muncy. *(MR. MUNCY Exits, grudgingly.)*

DR. KITCHENER. No doubt you found Mr. Muncy a bit backward with his night-school Freudianism.

HUGO. Huh?

DR. KITCHENER. You're an intelligent young man, Hugo—I wouldn't say this if you weren't. I've seen your I.Q., which is higher than Mr. Muncy's, believe me. Between you and me, Mr. Muncy's understanding of the human soul is 40 years out of date. Do you know what the word "psychiatrist" means?

HUGO. A doctor.

DR. KITCHENER. Yes, but what kind of doctor?

HUGO. A head doctor.

DR. KITCHENER. No, not quite. It comes from two Greek words meaning a doctor of the soul. That's all right, though; there are many things I don't know that you probably do know. Isn't that right?

HUGO. I guess.

DR. KITCHENER. Don't say "I guess"—of *course* there are. You probably know everything about sports, for example.

HUGO. No, I don't know too much about sports.

DR. KITCHENER. Well, I don't know anything!

HUGO. Nothing?

DR. KITCHENER. Not a thing.

HUGO. Well then, maybe you know a little less than I do.

DR. KITCHENER. *(after a beat) Any*way... A psychiatrist, as I was saying, is a doctor of the soul. You see, your soul can get sick sometimes just like your body. What would that mean to you, Hugo—to have a sick soul? Don't you want to talk to me, Hugo?

HUGO. Yeah. I'm thinking.

DR. KITCHENER. Let me help you out a little bit, then. Sometimes people begin to say to themselves, "I don't deserve to be happy like other people because I'm really not a very nice person." And why do they think they're not very nice? Well, maybe because their parents used to say, "Hugo..."—or George or Mary or any other name— "you're a bad boy, bad boy." You'd be surprised how many parents nowadays say all kinds of damaging things like that to their children. And the child starts to think, "Since Mom and Dad are always telling me how bad I am, I must *be* bad. There must be something about me that's not quite right." But the thing is, we're *all* all right; it's just that sometimes the soul gets sick, and then we need a soul doctor to find out where those bad feelings came from, and to get rid of them. Do you understand?

Hugo. Uh-uh.

Dr. Kitchener. What don't you understand?

Hugo. Well, my parents never told me I was bad, but I always knew that I was never as good as I wanted to be.

Dr. Kitchener. Well! That's because somebody or something made you feel bad about yourself. What we have to do is find out why, and then make you feel all better.

Hugo. Saint Augustine said that even when he was a baby less than a day old he was a sinner.

Dr. Kitchener. Saint Augustine was a very sick man. Where in the world did you come across *that* bit of information?

Hugo. In the Confessions.

Dr. Kitchener. You *read* the Confessions of Saint Augustine?

Hugo. It was in the library here. If Saint Augustine was a very sick man, does that mean that he wasn't all right?

Dr. Kitchener. No, I wouldn't say that. It simply means that he was in desperate need of professional help.

Hugo. That's what he says: that he needed God's help, right from the time he was born.

Dr. Kitchener. Hugo, *God* is not a professional. Do you actually believe in God?

Hugo. Sure. I believe in one God, Father Almighty,

Creator of heaven and earth...

DR. KITCHENER. Don't put me on, okay? I don't like that.

HUGO. I'm not putting you on. I mean, from what I know about God, it makes more sense to believe in *Him* than in anybody else.

DR. KITCHENER. I'm beginning to see what Mr. Muncy was talking about. You sound to me like a very conflicted young man.

HUGO. I am? I thought I was all right.

DR. KITCHENER. So did I. You don't see God, do you?

HUGO. No.

DR. KITCHENER. Thank God!

HUGO. But of course He sees me.

DR. KITCHENER. Right. No messages? Personal communications?

HUGO. No. That's what I keep hoping for, but it never happens. I just have to be patient.

DR. KITCHENER. I think I can still help you, then.

HUGO. To see God?

DR. KITCHENER. No! To see clearly. To see yourself. To find out why you can't get in touch with your true feelings—why you have to hide behind the defense of religion. To realize what you want for yourself. Success, right? Isn't that what we all want, when it comes right down to it? To feel that we've fought the good fight and made a success of ourselves? Honest to God, Hugo, you can do it. You've got the background, the intelligence. Don't throw it away. And don't give me this God crap. You have a chance to make something of yourself!

(The LIGHTS suddenly go out on everything except HUGO, who speaks to the audience.)

HUGO. This was when it happened. To this day it makes me kind of weak at the knees when I think about it, but you'll see what I mean.

(The LIGHTS come up on the scene again. The VOICE OF GOD is heard from above.)

VOICE OF GOD. Who is this that darkens counsel by words without knowledge?
DR. KITCHENER. What?! Hugo, did you do that?
HUGO. No, ma'am.
DR. KITCHENER. Well, what *was* it?
HUGO. It was a voice.
DR. KITCHENER. Where did it come from? Is there a public address system in here? Answer me, Hugo! what kind of a game do you think you're playing? Answer me, God damn it!

(A loud rumble of THUNDER is heard; she grabs at her heart and falls over on the floor. HUGO kneels at her body as the LIGHTS go down and the CHOIR reappears.)

SOLOIST.
SAINT HUGO HEARD JEHOVAH
AND PONDERED WHAT HE SAID.
JEHOVAH HEARD A SACRILEGE
AND STRUCK THE DOCTOR DEAD.

CHOIR.
SAINT HUGO, OH, SAINT HUGO,
WHY WILL WE NEVER LEARN?
SAINTS ARE BORN TO LEAD THE WAY
AND NEVER TO RETURN.
SAINT HUGO, OH, SAINT HUGO.

(BLACKOUT.)

END OF SCENE 2

SCENE 3

MR. DEPEW appears in a SPOTLIGHT.

MR. DEPEW. My son Hugo had a very happy childhood, contrary to what you might expect if you read that two-bit unauthorized biography that came out right after his death. I admit that before he started to make it big as a saint—which was a profession that I didn't even know existed before he got into it—I used to be kind of worried about him. I mean, there he was, 20 years old, and he never went out of the house. His mother said to him...

(A SPOTLIGHT comes up on MRS. DEPEW.)

Mrs. Depew. Hugo honey, maybe you'd like to go down to the malt shop or something and meet a few nice girls. Wouldn't that be nice?

(A SPOTLIGHT comes up on HUGO. As he begins talking all the LIGHTS come up on the livingroom of the DePew home, and the three of them assume their places in the room. The year is 1962. HUGO is trying to read a book.)

Hugo. I don't think there is a malt shop anymore. They turned it into a discotheque.
Mrs. Depew. Well, that's even nicer, isn't it? You used to like popular music so much. Wouldn't you like to go down to the discotheque and dance, sometime?
Hugo. No.
Mr. Depew. I used to like to dance. When I was your age, Hugo, I used to go out dancing three or four nights of the week. I used to go out after work. You'd think I'd be tired after working all day, but not me.
Mrs. Depew. I used to work, too, when I was Hugo's age.
Mr. Depew. I know you did. Most people do. Some people go to college, but most people work.
Mrs. Depew. Teddy Kenton works. His mother told me that he has a very good position in the post office. And he's only 18!
Mr. Depew. Only 18 and working in the post office!
Mrs. Depew. In a very good position. And he's engaged, too.

MR. DEPEW. Little Teddy Kenton?
MRS. DEPEW. Well, he's 18. At 18 you're not so little. You're ready to go out and work.
MR. DEPEW. Yes, that's right.

(The LIGHTS go out on everything except HUGO, who speaks to the audience.)

HUGO. One thing I'll say for my parents: they never pressured me to go out and get a job. I think this was because I was their only child, and besides, my mother was kind of scared of me after the cantaloupe business. Sometimes I got the impression they'd like me to meditate a little less and go out and have some fun like the other kids, but on the whole I was very happy that I hadn't managed to blow them up.

(The LIGHTS come up again on the livingroom.)

MRS. DEPEW. Hugo, where did you get that shirt you're wearing?
HUGO. I made it.
MRS. DEPEW. You made it? Is that what the kids are wearing nowadays: home made shirts? It doesn't look very comfortable.
HUGO. It's not. That's the point.
MR. DEPEW. It looks like that old horsehair sofa I threw out last winter.
MRS. DEPEW. Edgar! What a thing to say. I'm sure it looks very nice, to people who are Hugo's age.
MR. DEPEW. Yeah, well, if they want to wear

that kind of shirt when it's 98 degrees out, that's okay with me. But if it made me sweat like Hugo—who can't afford to sweat, since he's down to 132 pounds—I'd get rid of it pretty fast, even if it *was* the fashionable thing to wear.

MRS. DEPEW. 132 pounds! Is that right, Hugo?

HUGO. Huh?

MRS. DEPEW. How much do you weigh?

HUGO. 132 pounds.

MRS. DEPEW. Well, that's criminal. And you know why it is, don't you? It's because of your eating habits, young man.

HUGO. Yeah, I guess.

MRS. DEPEW. What have you had to eat today?

HUGO. This is Friday.

MRS. DEPEW. I know it's Friday; what does *that* mean?

HUGO. I don't eat on Friday.

MRS. DEPEW. You don't eat? Edgar, your son says he doesn't eat on Friday. Did you ever hear anything like that before in your life?

MR. DEPEW. Yeah, well, as long as he makes up for it on Saturday.

MRS. DEPEW. Makes up for it? Edgar, look at him! He weighs a hundred and 32 pounds! You could stuff your face all day long and you wouldn't *begin* to make up for being 50 pounds underweight. I know it's supposed to be hep to be thin—or hip: which is it?—but my goodness! Hugo, I am giving a call right this minute to Chicken Delight.

HUGO. I'm not hungry.

MRS. DEPEW. Well, of course not. People who starve themselves end up without any appetite at all. Look at those people in the Near East or wherever it is. We send them Care packages of good American food, and they don't even want to eat it. And why not? Certainly it tastes better than what they're used to, but suddenly they're just not hungry anymore. There was a picture in the paper of a 5-year-old child in Pakistan or someplace, just staring at a slice of Wonder Bread like it wasn't even food. Is that what you want to come to? Hugo? Do you want to lose your appetite entirely?

HUGO. I wish I could, but I don't think I'm up to it yet. Last Friday I ate a carrot.

MRS. DEPEW. A carrot? A single carrot? Hugo honey, when your mother was on her diet she ate two bunches of carrots a day. And I lost ten pounds in two weeks. At the rate you're going you'll be dead by December. There won't even be anything left to bury.

MR. DEPEW. Now, now. I'm sure that Hugo has some perfectly good reason for not eating on Fridays, and once we hear it we'll understand. Isn't that so?

HUGO. Well, yeah.

MR. DEPEW. And what is it?

HUGO. Well, I'll put it in terms of a parable.

MRS. DEPEW. A what?

HUGO. A parable.

MR. DEPEW. That's like a story.

HUGO. Yeah. Well, you see, there was this professional athlete who wanted to be able to run faster than anyone in the world...

MR. DEPEW. I knew it! He's in training!

HUGO. No—it's a parable. It doesn't really mean what it says.

MR. DEPEW. That's like in church.

HUGO. Right. Well, he practiced and practiced, and since it was the one thing in the world that he wanted more than anything else, he got very good at it. In fact, he got so good that he *did* run faster than everyone else.

MRS. DEPEW. Well, that was a nice story, but I don't see what it...

HUGO. It's not done—because he didn't stop trying to run faster and faster, even when there was no one else to beat. And he kept setting new records year after year, until people started calling him a show off and asking him why he didn't retire or something.

MR. DEPEW. Why didn't he? I mean, where you make the money is in the competition, right? Did they pay him for setting a new world's record every year?

HUGO. No. People were ready to pay him to stop, because he was taking all the fun out of it for all the other athletes, who couldn't run nearly as fast. So after he set the one minute mile...

MR. DEPEW. Jesus!

HUGO. ...this big group of people came to him and told him to stop, because he was ruining everything. They were proud of him and all, but the other runners were getting really mad, and a lot of them gave up the sport in disgust because they figured what's the use?

MRS. DEPEW. So what happened?

HUGO. They killed him.

MRS. DEPEW. Oh. Couldn't they have just put him away?

MR. DEPEW. Or crippled him, or something?

HUGO. No.

MRS. DEPEW. It would have been the humane thing to do—putting him away. Honestly, Edgar, you don't *cripple* somebody like that. He was a champion. He just didn't know when to quit.

MR. DEPEW. He should have retired when they asked him to.

MRS. DEPEW. That would have been better, sure.

HUGO. But he didn't want to retire. It gave him a lot of joy.

MR. DEPEW. Well, somebody should have sat down with him—like a close friend or somebody in the business...

HUGO. It was a *story*.

MR. DEPEW. ...and explained to him how it was counter-productive to keep on setting records like that without any purpose.

HUGO. No—y'see, there's no such person.

MR. DEPEW. What I would have done, if I'd been him, was take up some other sport after I'd won the world's championship in running. Like maybe the broad jump, or cross-country.

HUGO. But it's not real!

MRS. DEPEW. Or endorsed a line of sporting goods. That's what I'd do.

MR. DEPEW. Or tell jokes. Who's the guy on T.V. who can't sing or dance or anything—you know—

and just signed a million dollar contract with CBS? The big guy. That's how he got started: in the Olympics.

MRS. DEPEW. Oh, *I* know. He can sing a little. Besides, he's kinda cute.

MR. DEPEW. You call that singing?

MRS. DEPEW. Maybe we're not thinking about the same person. The one I'm thinking about is married to that starlet who gave the party where everybody got food poison from the hors d'oeuvres—or so they *said.*

MR. DEPEW. That's him. He can't sing for nuts.

MRS. DEPEW. Yes he can. Millie said it wasn't the hors d'oeuvres; it was drugs.

MR. DEPEW. I didn't know you could get food poison from drugs.

MRS. DEPEW. You can't, dummy.

MR. DEPEW. Was *he* there? *(HUGO Exits, unnoticed by either of his parents.)*

MRS. DEPEW. Sure. They said he had "food poison" worse than anyone else.

MR. DEPEW. I knew it. Look at him some time. His eyes are real beady, like he was on something.

MRS. DEPEW. You're kidding.

MR. DEPEW. No I'm not.

MRS. DEPEW. Beady?

MR. DEPEW. Like he was on something. Just look at him.

MRS. DEPEW. But he was an athlete!

MR. DEPEW. They all come to a bad end when they go into show business—everybody knows that. Too much easy living.

Mrs. Depew. I guess they *are* kind of beady. Hugo, do you think... Where's Hugo?

Mr. Depew. Went upstairs, I guess.

Mrs. Depew. Well, I hope he remembers to eat something. Maybe he'll go down to the malt shop later on. Honestly, Edgar—that boy is just skin and bone.

Mr. Depew. He's in training.

Mrs. Depew. He is?

Mr. Depew. That's what he said. Wants to be a professional runner.

Mrs. Depew. Oh, I get it. Well, how much does a professional runner have to weigh?

Mr. Depew. Don't ask me—ask Hugo.

Mrs. Depew. Well, I hope to God he's almost there.

(BLACKOUT.)

END OF SCENE 3

SCENE 4

A SOLOIST appears in a SPOTLIGHT. During his song we see a pantomime of the scene he describes.

Soloist.
AT DAWN EVERY MORNING SAINT HUGO ARISES
AND QUIETLY STARTS TO PRAY.
THE DEVIL APPEARS IN SO MANY DISGUISES;

WHAT WILL IT BE TODAY?

AT TIMES THROUGH THE WINDOW SAINT HUGO
  CAN SEE
A GIRL IN A NEGLIGEE.
SHE GIVES HIM A WINK AND SHE SHOWS HIM
  HER KNEE;
WHAT CAN HE DO BUT PRAY?

"OH LORD, I'M A SINNER,
OH LORD, I'M NOT STRONG.
I'VE GONE WITHOUT DINNER
FOR EVER SO LONG.
OH, GIVE ME THE STRENGTH TO RESIST IF YOU
  CAN,
AND MAKE ME A VIRTUOUS, VIRGINAL MAN."

HE LOOKS OUT THE WINDOW; SHE THROWS
  HIM A KISS;
AND THEN HE FORGETS TO PRAY.
THE DEVIL HAS STRATEGIES CRUELER THAN
  THIS;
WHAT WILL IT BE TODAY?

(BLACKOUT on SOLOIST. We see HUGO ringing the DOOR-BELL of an apartment. A female voice calls out.)

  VOICE. Who is it?
  HUGO. It's me. Your neighbor across the way.
  VOICE. Well, what do you want?
  HUGO. I want to talk to you.

VOICE. About what?
HUGO. About things.
VOICE. What things?
HUGO. Just about things in general.
VOICE. I can't talk now. I'm not dressed.
HUGO. I know.
VOICE. Oh, it's you! Why didn't you say so?

(SUSIE opens the door.)

SUSIE. So what took you so long?
HUGO. Can I come in?
SUSIE. Sure. *(HUGO Enters.)*
HUGO. I just wanted to drop by and say hello.
SUSIE. Hello!
HUGO. Hi. I guess I feel as if I know you already, since we're neighbors and...
SUSIE. ...and you seen me getting undressed every day for the past three weeks.
HUGO. I thought you were getting dressed.
SUSIE. At this time of the morning? You're shy, aren't you?
HUGO. Sort of.
SUSIE. What's your name?
HUGO. Hugo.
SUSIE. I'm Susie.
HUGO. Hi.
SUSIE. So what did you want to talk to me about, Hugo?
HUGO. Well, I wanted to ask you to please pull down your shade.

SUSIE. You did?

HUGO. Well, I mean, I can see you.

SUSIE. So don't look.

HUGO. But it's not that easy.

SUSIE. It isn't?

HUGO. I get up every morning at 5:30 and you're always there.

SUSIE. So pull *your* shade down.

HUGO. I didn't think about that. But what about other people?

SUSIE. Hugo, baby, you're the only one. I mean, who else is gonna get up at 5:30 all the time? What are you doing over there?

HUGO. Praying.

SUSIE. Yeah?

HUGO. Yeah. You ever talk to God? I mean, He's one person who really listens to ya.

SUSIE. Yeah? Well, I tell you what: you go home and pray for me, okay? 'Cause I could use it.

HUGO. That's what I thought—that maybe I could help you. I got the feeling you need help.

SUSIE. I *seen* this movie last week. Look, I make you a promise to keep my shade down from now on, how's that?

HUGO. Okay, but...

SUSIE. What?

HUGO. Can't we talk a little more? I didn't mean to offend you. I could see that you were a very friendly person, and I thought that we might... be friends.

SUSIE. Yeah?

HUGO. Yeah.

ACT I   ST. HUGO OF CENTRAL PARK

SUSIE. You wanna see where I live?
HUGO. Isn't this it?
SUSIE. No, I mean where I really live—in the bedroom.
HUGO. Oh, well... I guess I could take a look. It's not far, is it?
SUSIE. Right through that door.
HUGO. Well, I guess I'd like to see where you really live, all right.
SUSIE. Then come on, baby. What are you waiting for?

(As they go into the bedroom, the LIGHTS go out on everything except HUGO.)

HUGO. One thing that always puzzled me about people's attitude toward the saints was that they figured they never did anything wrong. This is also, it seems to me, why people tend to think that they're great folks to pray to but they wouldn't want to live with one. Now, I'm not proud of what happened with Susie, because it was like breaking training, in a way. But looking back on it now I can see that I was kind of hung up on my virginity at the time, and until I lost it I didn't really have a clear idea of what I was trying to resist.

(The LIGHTS go out and come up on the bedroom. SUSIE is in bed; HUGO is getting dressed.)

SUSIE. You gotta be kidding. Never?
HUGO. Never before this.

Susie. You mean you never had?
Hugo. No.
Susie. Well, why not?
Hugo. I wanted to be good.
Susie. Well, you *were,* baby. You were.

(The LIGHTS go out and come up on SUSIE speaking to the audience.)

Susie. Listen: at the start I thought, this is *some* trick. One thing you gotta watch out for in my business is a sickie. I'm laying on the bed watching him get undressed, and he takes off his coat, and then this shirt made out of an old doormat or something, and then I see these welts and bruises all over his body and I think "Uh-oh!" And there's this chain around his waist, see, with little points that stick into his skin. All of which doesn't add up to my idea of a good time. But wow, was it ever! I just wanna say that a good time was had by *all,* too; he liked it as much as I did, even though he didn't come back for more. Of course we all know he never had anybody else, so that puts me in a kind of unique position in Hugos' life: I was the first and last. It also had oughta put me in a pretty unique position when they make the movie about Hugo's life. I mean, who else could play *me,* right?

Anyway, things started really happening for me when I recognized his picture in the paper—which is kind of funny in itself, 'cause it was like three years later, and I glance at this story called "Modern Day Miracle Man," and whaddaya know? Something goes click inside my head, and I say to myself, "Susie, this is your very own personal weirdo!" So I happen to mention all this to a coupla people, and before I know it I get a call from the National Enquirer, and they offer me two thousand bucks for my exclusive story. What could be more terrific, right? Except it wasn't, and if anybody read "I Was Raped by the Miracle Man," I just wanna say that I'm sorry about it, but it wasn't my fault. Everything got all twisted. Especially about Hugo being into S & M and all that, 'cause the part about him asking me to beat him with the chain was completely made up by some sick magazine writer. I guess they thought it would sell more copies that way, which it probably did. And I guess people think that anybody who wants to be a saint has to be some kind of pervert. Not Hugo. I mean, sure he was weird, but when he said "I love you" it wasn't like... See, everybody says that. It's like what you gotta say. Thing is, with Hugo it was... well, maybe he really *did*. I mean, it's not impossible. I'm also sorry, since we're talking about this, that I ever made that quickie movie called "Kiss My Cross"—but I really needed the money and I think maybe Hugo would understand. I didn't have a chance to get to know him very well, but he seemed like a real understanding person, and if we ever meet again—which isn't very likely, considering where he is and where I'm gonna be—I think maybe he'd say he forgave me. I'd like to be able to say that he was the only man I ever loved, but that would be a lie, since we didn't really have time to get acquainted. But I will say this, and I mean it: he was the only man I ever gave it to for free.

(The LIGHTS go out on SUSIE and come up on SUSIE and

HUGO in her livingroom.)

SUSIE. Whaddaya mean you haven't got any money? Whaddaya think I am, your girl friend or something?

HUGO. I didn't know I had to pay.

SUSIE. You didn't know? Honest, baby, you gotta wise up a little. I mean, you're terrific, but so what when a girl has to pay the rent?

HUGO. Don't you have a job?

SUSIE. Yeah, I'm a free sample lady. I give out free samples.

HUGO. Well, don't you make any money at that?

SUSIE. Hugo, you're a nice kid, y'know?

HUGO. Thank you.

SUSIE. But a dumb one. So look... I'm gonna break the only rule I ever had and let you off.

HUGO. You are?

SUSIE. Yeah. You can remember me in your prayers.

HUGO. I will.

SUSIE. And baby?

HUGO. Yeah?

SUSIE. This is crazy.

HUGO. What?

SUSIE. I'm not gonna pull my shade down, either.

(They stand looking at each other as the SOLOIST appears and sings.)

SOLOIST.
WE ALL HAVE OUR MORALS; WE ALL HAVE IDEALS;

WE ALL HAVE BEEN KNOWN TO STRAY.
THE DEVIL'S A MASTER OF MANY APPEALS;
WHAT CAN WE DO BUT PRAY?

(BLACKOUT.)

END OF SCENE 4

SCENE 5

MR. and MRS. DEPEW at home. The year is 1964.

MRS. DEPEW. I don't like it. It's going too far. I can see taking care of them, especially if it's a real, honest-to-goodness job, but I can't see going to live with them. Hugo is 22 years old, and he ought to be doing something more constructive with his time. If he wants to do social work, he should do it with human beings.

MR. DEPEW. It's a phase, just a phase.

MRS. DEPEW. Hugo's whole life is a phase! Hugo has been in a phase, according to you, ever since he started to talk. When does it end?—that's what I want to know. When does he come out of this phase of his and turn into a normal American boy?

MR. DEPEW. He likes them. And it gets him out of the house.

MRS. DEPEW. Well, that's pretty sad—that we've come to that. In order to get your son out of the house, you're willing to let him go live with the pigeons in Central Park. Where does he sleep?

MR. DEPEW. Under the bushes, he says.

MRS. DEPEW. Under the bushes. My son Hugo sleeps under the bushes in Central Park.

MR. DEPEW. He says the pigeons keep him warm.

MRS. DEPEW. Do the pigeons protect him from the muggers, too? Edgar, I thought I'd be the last person ever to say this, but that boy is disturbed. Nobody sleeps under the bushes in Central Park unless they're disturbed.

MR. DEPEW. It's a new world, Emily.

MRS. DEPEW. Not that new. I was talking to Loretta down at the beauty shop and I said, what do you think of these new fads like cutting little crosses in the palms of your hands?—and she gave me a look like I was out of my mind. She asked me where I heard about that, and I told her my husband said it was a new fad. She said you were putting me on. Now, Loretta is 19 and she *knows*.

MR. DEPEW. She's probably just not with it, like Hugo.

MRS. DEPEW. With it? I'm up to here with being with it. If it's with it to act like Hugo, the human race is in big trouble.

MR. DEPEW. That's why they act like that: because of the bomb and the war and everything else. If I'd had all that to contend with when I was a boy, I just might have gone and lived with the pigeons, too.

MRS. DEPEW. Well, Central Park was safer when you

were a boy. And anyway, Hugo doesn't have to contend with the war. They don't draft people out of a reformatory.

Mr. Depew. But he has to contend with it as a moral issue

Mrs. Depew. Well, so do I, but you don't see me coming home covered with pigeon droppings, do you? Or begging for money to buy bread on 57th Street.

Mr. Depew. He wants to be independent.

Mrs. Depew. Edgar, I don't want to talk about it. But if *your* best friend in the world had been walking down 57th Street and had been approached by an emaciated person covered with pigeon droppings and asked for money to buy bread, and if that person had turned out to be *your* son—which it did—you wouldn't be so calm about it.

Mr. Depew. You can't blame Hugo just because he happens to hurt your pride.

Mrs. Depew. Hurts my pride! Of *course* he hurts my pride—you make it sound like nothing! Let me tell you something, Edgar: my pride is very important to me, and I'm not ashamed of that fact, either. Say what you like, but there isn't a woman in the world who wouldn't die a little if she had to tell her best friend that her only son had become a pigeon person.

Mr. Depew. Pride goeth before a fall.

Mrs. Depew. You sound just like Hugo. Why don't you go and live in the park, too?

Mr. Depew. Emily...

Mrs. Depew. It's a new world, Edgar.

Mr. Depew. It's just his way of asserting himself, that's all. Some kids go out and picket...

MRS. DEPEW. I know, I know.

MR. DEPEW. ...and some kids go live in the park. It's the thing to do.

MRS. DEPEW. Really? Other kids, too?

MR. DEPEW. Of course.

MRS. DEPEW. Kids from better families?

MR. DEPEW. The best. We just gotta wait it out, that's all.

MRS. DEPEW. You don't understand how I suffer because of him.

MR. DEPEW. So what if he makes us suffer? You think that's something new? Let me tell you something, Emily: kids are *born* to make their parents suffer; it's the will of God. That's what being a parent is all about.

MRS. DEPEW. Amen, Edgar. Amen.

(BLACKOUT.)

END OF SCENE 5

SCENE 6

The CHOIR Enters in procession. PIGEON NOISES are heard in the background.

CHOIR.
ALLE, ALLE, ALLELU!

ACT I   ST. HUGO OF CENTRAL PARK   41

HEAR THE HAPPY PIGEONS COO.
ALLELUIA! ALLELU!
HEAR THE HAPPY PIGEONS COO.
ALLELUIA! ALLELU!
   SOLOIST. *(recitativo)*
OH, SAINT HUGO, WE REMEMBER YOUR HOLY
  WORDS:
"YOU CAN DO WHAT YOU LIKE WITH ME,
BUT DON'T MESS AROUND WITH THE BIRDS."
   CHOIR.
ALLE, ALLE, ALLELU!
HEAR THE HAPPY PIGEONS COO.
LET THE PIGEONS SING IT TO YA:
ALLE, ALLE, ALLELUIA!

(The CHOIR Exits, singing. The song fades as the LIGHTS come up on HUGO, holding a pigeon.)

  HUGO. People got into all kinds of arguments, after I got famous, about the fact that I went to live with the pigeons in the park instead of doing something more civic-minded like working in a ghetto or helping out at a hospital or something. Some people said it was a good thing, and some people said it was a bad thing. But the truth is, it just never occurred to me to do anything else. Ever since Dr. Kitchener died, I'd been praying to God all the time, hoping that I'd hear Him speak again. And then one day, all of a sudden, it happened. I guess it was about the best day in my life so far. I was on my way to the hardware store to buy some more sandpaper for my bed. And I heard this voice that said, "Get on the IND uptown express at York Street and change to the KK at Fourth."

So I took the KK and the voice said, "Get off at 57th and go into the park." So I did. And then all these pigeons came at me, and the same voice says, "Look at the birds of the air; they neither sow nor reap nor gather into barns." And I was thinking about how true that was, because when you try to imagine them doing any of those things, especially in Manhattan, you can see right away that it wouldn't work. And then it occurred to me that somebody ought to make things a little easier for them. Now, the people who said I should have worked in a ghetto instead seemed to feel that I was wasting my time. They said that the pigeons always managed to survive anyway, and besides, people are more important. Those are pretty good arguments, but the thing is, that's not what I was told to do. Well, anyway, as things worked out, I think I probably did the right thing.

(SCENE: The LIGHTS come up around HUGO to reveal that he is at the Bethesda Fountain in Central Park. It is spring, 1964. HUGO sits on the edge of the fountain and begins to make a splint for the pigeon out of ice cream sticks. JOHN and MARTHA, a middle-aged couple, are passing by.)

HUGO. *(to the pigeon:)* What I don't understand is why you got in the fight in the first place. You and Ozzie always seemed to be real pals.

MARTHA. *(to JOHN:)* Did you hear that?

JOHN. What?

MARTHA. Sometimes I think everybody in this whole goddamn park just sits around and talks to himself.

JOHN. He's not talking to himself. He's talking to the

bird. Come on.

MARTHA. Well, it's a shame—a young man like that. What'd he say?

JOHN. Who cares? The thing to do is not get close enough so he starts talking to *us*.

MARTHA. He's filthy! Look what he's wearing.

JOHN. Martha, people who talk to pigeons aren't usually too chic. Come on, will you?

HUGO. *(to JOHN and MARTHA:)* I don't suppose you happen to have a piece of gauze or something?

JOHN. No. Martha!

MARTHA. It's got a broken leg.

JOHN. Come on.

MARTHA. He's making a splint out of ice cream sticks.

JOHN. *(to HUGO:)* You want a dollar?

HUGO. I don't think it would work. What I need is a piece of gauze or a handkerchief or something.

MARTHA. Poor little birdie. I've got a handkerchief.

JOHN. Martha!

MARTHA. *(producing a handkerchief)* Little birdie-wirdie broke his leggie-weggie.

JOHN. Martha, we're going to be late.

MARTHA. Where are we going?

JOHN. Home.

MARTHA. How can we be late getting home?

JOHN. Martha! *(to HUGO:)* How about a five dollar bill?

HUGO. That wouldn't be any better. The handkerchief's okay, if I can rip it up.

MARTHA. Go ahead. *(HUGO tears the handkerchief into strips.)*

MARTHA. He looks kind of weak.

HUGO. She. She'll be okay, if she stays away from Ozzie for a while.

MARTHA. Who's Ozzie?

JOHN. You had to ask.

HUGO. Ozzie's the one who beat her up.

MARTHA. Oh, my God! You mean there are people who go around beating up pigeons? Isn't there enough violence in this city already?

HUGO. Ozzie is a pigeon. He's her boyfriend. *(to pigeon:)* Now, bite your beak. This is going to hurt. *(JOHN starts humming.)*

MARTHA. Why are you humming?

JOHN. Was I humming?

MARTHA. Yes. It might disturb her. *(to HUGO:)* What's her name?

JOHN. Oh, for God's sake!

HUGO. Rosalinda.

MARTHA. What a pretty name!

HUGO. It's because she has kind of a rosy color here, on her throat.

MARTHA. Well, why did Ozzie beat her up, if he's her boyfriend?

HUGO. I don't know. Ozzie seems to get possessed sometimes, and he goes around picking fights. He's the only one who won't coo when we say our prayers.

JOHN. Martha, honey, please. Please, please, please. Let's go aitch oh em ee.

MARTHA. Just a minute. *(to HUGO:)* When do you say your prayers?

HUGO. When we're all together.

MARTHA. Yes, but...

(JUDY and ELROY, two young people, pass by. ELROY is blind and wears a camera around his neck; JUDY is leading him.)

JUDY. *(to ELROY:)* Ooh! Take a picture of that! Quick, Elroy!

ELROY. What is it?

JUDY. It's a guy with a sick pigeon.

ELROY. Well, point me in the right direction.

JUDY. You *are* in the right direction. Just hold up the camera and press the button.

JOHN. Martha, quick! They're gonna take your picture!

MARTHA. Well, so what?

JOHN. You don't want a record of this, do you?

(ELROY snaps the picture.)

JUDY. That'll be beautiful.

ELROY. What'll it look like?

JUDY. Well, there's this real dirty looking guy, and he's putting a... *(to HUGO:)* Excuse me.

HUGO. Yeah?

JUDY. What do you call that thing you made out of ice cream sticks?

HUGO, JOHN & MARTHA. Splint.

JUDY. Right. And he's putting a splint made out of ice cream sticks on the pigeon's leg. I bet you could sell this picture to the papers, because it's real human interest.

JOHN. *(to JUDY:)* Now, wait a minute!

JUDY. *(to ELROY:)* Oh, yeah. And there are two old people looking on.

MARTHA. Old people!

JUDY. *(to ELROY:)* It's a good thing you got this picture a minute ago, because now their expressions have turned real ugly.

JOHN. What's the meaning of this? Who said you could take our picture?

JUDY. Who said we couldn't?

MARTHA. How can he take a picture, anyway? He's...

ELROY. *(facing the wrong direction)* You got something against blind people taking your picture, lady?

JUDY. She's over here, Elroy.

ELROY. Oh. *(facing MARTHA)* You got something against blind people taking your picture, lady?

MARTHA. No, I... Well, you've got to admit it's an unusual hobby for a... Well, sighted people usually...

ELROY. Ain't no hobby. I'm a free lance photographer.

MARTHA. Oh. Well.

ELROY. Hobby, shit! You see this camera?

MARTHA. Yes, I... Very nice camera.

ELROY. Only pros got cameras like this.

MARTHA. Well. It's certainly very nice.

ELROY. Four hundred bucks, lady. It's a fuckin' Hasselblad.

MARTHA. My! Well, I suppose you were a professional photographer even before you...went blind.

ELROY. I always been blind, lady. I was born blind.

JUDY. Elroy is in our arts program at the Institute for the Blind.

MARTHA. I see. Well!

JOHN. Gotta go now, Martha.

MARTHA. Hmm?

JUDY. Elroy, you should see this pigeon. It's so cute. It has this pink neck.

JOHN. *(to JUDY:)* Watch out!

JUDY. What? Why?

JOHN. Don't touch it! It might be diseased!

HUGO. No, she's all right. It's just her leg.

JOHN. How do you know? I wouldn't touch you, either.

MARTHA. John! What a thing to say!

JOHN. Well, would you? He looks like he lives with them.

ELROY. Gee, what does he look like?

JUDY. Well, he's real thin and like I say, real dirty. His hair is all stringy and there's... Yuchh!

ELROY. What's the matter?

JUDY. There's pigeon shit all over his clothes.

ELROY. Wow! Lemme take another. Am I facing the right way?

JUDY. Yes.

ELROY. Is he smiling?

JUDY. *(to HUGO:)* Could you smile for him, please? *(to ELROY:)* Now he is. Get in a little closer. Okay—there. *(ELROY snaps the picture.)*

ELROY. Let me feel him.

JUDY. Elroy, I don't think you wanna do that.

JOHN. Don't do it, Elroy. *(ELROY lunges toward HUGO but grabs MARTHA instead.)*

JUDY. That's the lady!

ELROY. Sorry.

(A POLICEMAN, who has been observing them, comes over.)

POLICEMAN. *(to MARTHA:)* These people bothering you, ma'am?

MARTHA. No, that's all right. You see, he's blind, and he wanted to touch the boy with the pigeon.

POLICEMAN. Oh. I wouldn't do that, if I was him.

HUGO. It's all right, officer.

POLICEMAN. *(to HUGO:)* You keep outa this. I've had just about enough outa you.

MARTHA. What did he do?

POLICEMAN. Do?! Lady, look at him!

MARTHA. So?

POLICEMAN. When you look like that, you don't *hafta* do anything. It's a crime just to sit in a public place.

JOHN. He's up to something, too. I offered him money and he wouldn't take it.

POLICEMAN. *(to HUGO:)* Up to your old tricks again, huh? Okay—you're coming with me. *(to JOHN:)* Will you file a complaint, saying he wouldn't take your money?

JOHN. You bet.

MARTHA. John! He didn't *do* anything.

POLICEMAN. *(to HUGO:)* I said come on.

ELROY. Wait! I wanna touch him! *(He lunges toward HUGO and lands on top of him.)*

MARTHA. The pigeon!

JUDY. Elroy, you've hurt the pigeon!

HUGO. Rosalinda? Rosalinda, where are you? *(finding her unharmed)* She's okay. Don't worry, everybody. she's okay.

MARTHA. Thank God!

JOHN. *(to MARTHA:)* Now can we please get out of here?

ELROY. Holy shit!

JUDY. *(while helping ELROY to his feet)* What is it?

ELROY. Holy shit!

JUDY. What *is* it, Elroy?

ELROY. Holy shit!

JUDY. Don't just keep saying that. What is it?

ELROY. Holy shit!

MARTHA. *(to JUDY:)* Is he like this often?

JUDY. I don't know what's the matter. Elroy!

ELROY. Wait a minute. Wait a minute. Wait *a* minute. Am I wearing dark glasses, maybe?

JUDY. Of course you are; you know that.

ELROY. Take 'em off, take 'em off, take 'em off! *(JUDY removes his glasses.)*

ELROY. Holy shit!

POLICEMAN. If he wasn't blind, I'd run *him* in, too. Watch your language!

ELROY. He did it! He did it! Holy shit, he really did it!

JUDY. Who did what?

ELROY. *(pointing at HUGO)* *He* did it!

JUDY. *(thunderstruck)* Elroy! You pointed! Holy shit!

ELROY. He did it!

JUDY. He did it!

POLICEMAN. Aw, shut up!

MARTHA. Won't anybody tell me what he did?

JUDY. I'll tell you! I'll tell you! He... holy shit!

(The CHOIR is heard offstage.)

Choir.
ALLELU-IA!

(BLACKOUT.)

END OF ACT I

ACT II
SCENE 1

The LIGHTS come up on HUGO, surrounded by four REPORTERS.

REPORTERS. *(ad lib)* Hey, kid, how'd ya do it? What's the story? Hey, Hugo! Hugo!

(The REPORTERS freeze in position and the LIGHTS dim on them. HUGO remains in a SPOTLIGHT, and he speaks to the audience.)

HUGO. I want to get one thing straight. I never did walk on water, and the fact that I ever tried just goes to show how mixed up I was after all the publicity about Elroy and how he wasn't blind anymore. Four thousand people just stood there on the beach at Atlantic City and watched while I nearly drowned. Maybe they thought I was walking underwater, I don't know; but finally some lifeguard was smart enough to swim out and save me. Anyway, it was real humiliating, and I'm sure that's the way God wanted it. The weird part of it is that a lot of people seem to think I did walk on water, even though I didn't. What I see as the greatest sin I ever committed was trying to prove myself to anybody else but God. I guess I was always trying to prove myself at the start. I mean like the hair shirt business seems like kid stuff to me now, but at the time it helped me to see that being comfortable was kind of a distraction. People get hooked on being comfortable, y'know—and pretty soon that means they gotta stop thinking about how they want to be better people, and start thinking about how they wanta be better *off.* What I tried to do was just find all my comfort in God. But things got real difficult when it turned out I had these powers, see, and I thought if I could help people I guess I should. I guessed that's what God would want. But it didn't turn out to be quite that simple.

(The LIGHTS come up again on the reanimated RE-PORTERS.)

REPORTER 1. How'd you do it, Hugo? How'd it happen?

HUGO. It doesn't make any sense. I didn't do anything. He just fell on top of me—I mean the blind guy. I was sitting there with Rosalinda...

REPORTER 2. Is that your girl?

HUGO. She's one of my pigeons.

REPORTER 2. You play the field, do you?

HUGO. Huh?

REPORTER 2. You have more than one "pigeon?"

HUGO. Oh, yeah. I have about four hundred of them now.

REPORTER 1. Wow! What an angle! The saint's a super stud!

REPORTER 3. *(to No. 1:)* I think he means real pigeons.

REPORTER 1. Yeah? Who asked you? Hey, Hugo, you

don't mean real pigeons, do ya?

REPORTER 3. Hugo, how long have you lived with the pigeons?

HUGO. About six months. I don't know what they're doing right now, because I usually have their food all ready for them by the time they get back from flying around all day.

REPORTER 1. *(to No. 2:)* Jesus! He means real pigeons.

REPORTER 2. *(to No. 1:)* So who needs an angle?

REPORTER 4. You ever heal anybody else, Hugo?

HUGO. Not that I know of. But I didn't even...

REPORTER 3. To what do you attribute your ability to cure blindness?

HUGO. I don't know. Maybe he wasn't really blind.

REPORTER 2. He was blind, all right. We checked.

HUGO. Well, then, it must have been an act of God. I was just *there*.

REPORTER 1. Hey, Hugo, I got a bad back.

HUGO. I'm sorry.

REPORTER 3. *(to No. 1:)* Will you quit?

REPORTER 1. Hold on a minute. *(to HUGO:)* Is it okay if I touch you?

HUGO. Huh? Sure, go ahead. *(REPORTER 1 touches HUGO.)*

REPORTER 3. *(to No. 1:)* So?

REPORTER 1. Huh? Oh, I won't be able to tell until it starts acting up again.

REPORTER 3. Moron!

REPORTER 4. Idiot!

REPORTER 1. *(screaming)* Aaaaaaaaahhh!

REPORTERS 2, 3 & 4. What is it?
REPORTER 1. AAAAAAHHHH!
REPORTERS 2, 3 & 4. What is it?
REPORTER 1. I can't move.
REPORTER 2. What?
REPORTER 1. I'm paralyzed, dammit! Do something!
HUGO. Oh, no! Oh God, please!
REPORTER 4. *(falling to his knees)* Holy Mother of God!
REPORTER 1. *(to No. 4:)* Don't pray—do something! Help me! Get me a doctor!
REPORTER 2. *(to No. 3:)* Get him a doctor!
REPORTER 3. You get him a doctor. You think I'm gonna miss out on a story like this?
HUGO. Isn't anybody gonna help him?
REPORTER 1. *(to HUGO:)* You punk! You wise ass punk! You... *(He continues moving his mouth, but no sounds can be heard.)*
REPORTER 2. What's he saying?
REPORTER 3. I don't know. I can't hear anything.
REPORTER 2. *(to No. 1:)* Harry! Harry, what happened?

(REPORTER 1 seems to be screaming at them, but he's mute. REPORTER 4 is still on his knees, praying.)

HUGO. I'll get a doctor.
REPORTER 3. He lost his voice! How can you quote somebody who lost his voice?
REPORTER 2. *(to No. 1:)* Speak up, Harry! *(HUGO runs off.)*

ACT II   ST. HUGO OF CENTRAL PARK   55

REPORTER 2. *(calling after HUGO)* Hey, come back here!
REPORTER 4. Hail, Mary, full of grace...
REPORTER 3. *(to No. 4:)* Can it! *(to No. 2:)* Where's the kid?
REPORTER 2. He went to get a doctor.
REPORTER 3. I wouldn't touch that kid with a ten foot pole. You think he really did it?
REPORTER 2. I don't know. First the blind guy, then Harry...
REPORTER 3. Yeah, but Harry got zapped!
REPORTER 2. Well, y'know Harry wasn't too cool about the whole thing. I mean he was kind of asking for it. *(REPORTER 1 starts screaming at them, noiselessly.)*
REPORTER 2. *(to No. 1:)* Well, you were. Honest to God, Harry, I'd think you'd have better sense. A bad back! What kinda crap is that? This kid's the real thing.

(HUGO comes running back in.)

REPORTER 2. *(to HUGO:)* Don't touch me!
HUGO. They're calling a doctor. I said to send an ambulance.
REPORTER 2. Oh yeah? Terrific.
REPORTER 4. *(from the floor)* Hugo!
HUGO. Yeah?
REPORTER 4. Hugo!
HUGO. What is it?
REPORTER 4. Hugo!
REPORTER 2. *(to No. 4:)* Get a hold of yourself, will you?

HUGO. What does he want?
REPORTER 3. Who knows? I don't understand *anything* anymore.
REPORTER 2. *(to HUGO:)* How'd you do it?
HUGO. Do what?
REPORTER 2. Zap Harry like that.
HUGO. I didn't zap Harry! I didn't do anything! *(to No. 1:)* I'm sorry, Harry. Forgive me!
REPORTER 2. Look, kid, he deserved it. *(REPORTER 1 starts screaming noiselessly again.)*
REPORTER 2. *(to No. 1:)* Shut up, Harry.
REPORTER 3. *(to No. 1:)* Yeah. Keep it down, will ya?
REPORTER 2. You can tell us, Hugo. We're your friends.
HUGO. What about Harry?
REPORTERS 2 & 3. What about him?
HUGO. Well, I thought maybe we could make him comfortable or something. Maybe if I can help him to lie down... *(HUGO goes toward REPORTER 1, who responds with a look of horror.)*
REPORTER 4. Hugo!
HUGO. Yeah?
REPORTER 4. Hugo!
REPORTER 2. *(to No. 4:)* Spit it out!
REPORTER 4. I... I...
REPORTER 2. *(to No. 4:)* Come on! We haven't got all day.
HUGO. *(to No. 4:)* What is it?
REPORTER 4. Bless you. Bless you, Hugo.
REPORTER 3. Shit! Was that all?
HUGO. *(to No. 4:)* Get up, please! Don't bless me!

REPORTER 4. Our father, who art in heaven, hallowed be thy name. Thy kingdom come, thy will be done, on earth as it is in heaven...

HUGO. *(crying out, simultaneous with REPORTER 4)* Oh God, help me! Help me! What have I done?

(The LIGHTS fade out quickly on the scene as the CHOIR appears.)

CHOIR.
SAINT HUGO WAS A HEALER.
HE CURED THE HANDICAPPED.
THEIR HEARTS WERE FILLED WITH GLADNESS...
SOLOIST.
EXCEPT FOR THOSE HE ZAPPED.
CHOIR.
SAINT HUGO, OH, SAINT HUGO,
WHY WILL WE NEVER LEARN?
SAINTS ARE BORN TO LEAD THE WAY
AND SINNERS ARE BORN TO BURN.
SINNERS ARE BORN TO BURN.
SINNERS ARE BORN TO BURN.

(BLACKOUT.)

END OF SCENE 1

SCENE 2

When the LIGHTS come up we see HUGO and DR. OSCAR PETRICOFF at a medical research center in New York. NURSE NOBLE is standing by.

DR. PETRICOFF. You understand our purpose, Mr. DePew?

HUGO. Yeah, I do, Doctor, but...

DR. PETRICOFF. And you understand that the people you're about to meet have volunteered for this experiment? That no one has been forced to participate?

HUGO. Yeah, but...

DR. PETRICOFF. Quite frankly, a great many people are afraid to touch you, Mr. DePew. A lady said to me this morning she'd rather be blind than blind and paralyzed.

HUGO. Oh, sure. Me too.

DR. PETRICOFF. We all would, believe me. I know what you must be feeling...

HUGO. You do?

DR. PETRICOFF. ...and I want to reassure you that there's one purpose, and only one, behind all our work here at the Research Center, and that's to alleviate human suffering.

HUGO. Well, good, 'cause I really don't want to hurt anybody.

DR. PETRICOFF. Oh, don't worry about that. These people can't be hurt, Mr. DePew. They signed a release.

HUGO. A what?

DR. PETRICOFF. Miss Noble, will you bring in the first applicant, please? *(NURSE NOBLE Exits.)*

HUGO. They signed a what?

DR. PETRICOFF. Calm down, now. How are you feeling today?

HUGO. Awful. I haven't gotten much sleep in the past couple of days because of what happened to that poor reporter, and people keep asking me questions that I can't answer and besides all that I'm worried about my pigeons.

DR. PETRICOFF. Yes? Well, I'm sure they can take care of themselves.

HUGO. I'm not.

DR. PETRICOFF. They carry diseases, you know. While you're here, perhaps you should have a checkup.

HUGO. You want to examine me?

DR. PETRICOFF. Me? Well, actually... I was thinking one of my colleagues might.

(NURSE NOBLE returns with MR. PINCKNEY, a very old blind man.)

NURSE NOBLE. This is Mr. Pinckney, Doctor.

DR. PETRICOFF. How do you do, Mr. Pinckney?

MR. PINCKNEY. Is he here?

DR. PETRICOFF. Yes, he is. Mr. DePew, this is Mr. Pinckney. Would you like to... shake hands?

HUGO. Doctor, I...

MR. PINCKNEY. Hold it! First I want to show that I'm really blind.

DR. PETRICOFF. There's no need, Mr. Pinckney. I know that you're really blind.

MR. PINCKNEY. How?

DR. PETRICOFF. I have your file. It says you are.

MR. PINCKNEY. My file? I thought you were a man of science.

DR. PETRICOFF. I am.

MR. PINCKNEY. Then you're gonna want proof. Nurse!

NURSE NOBLE. Yes, Mr. Pinckney?

MR. PINCKNEY. Hold up a number of fingers in front of my face, but don't tell me how many. *(NURSE NOBLE looks questioningly at DR. PETRICOFF.)*

DR. PETRICOFF. Oh, go ahead, Miss Noble. *(She holds up three fingers in front of MR. PINCKNEY'S face.)*

NURSE NOBLE. All right. I'm holding them in front of your face.

MR. PINCKNEY. Now ask me how many there are.

NURSE NOBLE. Doctor?

DR. PETRICOFF. Get on with it.

NURSE NOBLE. How many fingers am I holding up, Mr. Pinckney?

MR. PINCKNEY. No idea! Can't see a damn thing!

DR. PETRICOFF. Well! I guess that doesn't leave any doubt. Now, if...

MR. PINCKNEY. Hold it!

DR. PETRICOFF. What is it?

MR. PINCKNEY. How do you know I'm not lying?

DR. PETRICOFF. Mr. Pinckney! *(To NURSE:)* Is he the

best you've got?
NURSE NOBLE. He was the first in line.
DR. PETRICOFF. Look, Mr. Pinckney, I'm a very busy man. Would you just shake hands with Mr. DePew here and get it over with?
HUGO. Doctor, I'm afraid.
DR. PETRICOFF. Now, there's nothing to be afraid of. Just come over here...
HUGO. I think he has to fall on me.
MR. PINCKNEY. Fall on you? They didn't tell me I had to fall on anybody.
DR. PETRICOFF. Let's just try it shaking hands, all right? *(HUGO very reluctantly shakes hands with MR. PINCKNEY.)*
HUGO. How do you do, Mr. Pinckney?
DR. PETRICOFF. *(to MR. PINCKNEY:)* Well?
MR. PINCKNEY. Very well, thank you. Never felt better in my life.
DR. PETRICOFF. How are you?
MR. PINCKNEY. I just told you.
DR. PETRICOFF. But can you see?
MR. PINCKNEY. Of course I can see. That's what I'm here for, isn't it?
DR. PETRICOFF. Prove it!
MR. PINCKNEY. Aha! Now you want proof. What kind of proof?
DR. PETRICOFF. Well, let me see. We have a number of tests... Miss Noble, hold up your fingers again. *(NURSE NOBLE holds up four fingers for MR. PINCKNEY.)*
MR. PINCKNEY. Lemme see... *(to NURSE NOBLE:)* Does this mean you're not married?

Dr. Petricoff. What?

Mr. Pinckney. No ring, bozo.

Nurse Noble. Doctor!

Mr. Pinckney. *(to NURSE NOBLE:)* I could really blow my disability check on somebody like you, sweetheart.

Dr. Petricoff. Just count the fingers, Pinckney!

Mr. Pinckney. Huh? Oh, four.

Hugo. That's right! Congratulations! *(HUGO reaches out to shake MR. PINCKNEY'S hand in congratulation, and everyone recoils; he withdraws his hand. NURSE NOBLE holds up two fingers.)*

Mr. Pinckney. Two!

Hugo. Gee, you're good at this! *(She holds up five fingers.)*

Mr. Pinckney. Five!

Nurse Noble. Doctor, he did it! He can see!

Mr. Pinckney. That's not all I can do, baby. What time d'you get off tonight?

Dr. Petricoff. That will do, Mr. Pinckney. Apparently we have some kind of a phenomenon here. Are you sure you were totally blind?

Mr. Pinckney. I told you to check me out! I told you! Now it's too late.

Hugo. Are you a religious man, Mr. Pinckney?

Mr. Pinckney. Huh?

Hugo. Do you believe in a greater power?

Mr. Pinckney. Ah, c'mon.

Nurse Noble. It's a miracle! A miracle!

Hugo. It was God who did this, y'know—not me.

Mr. Pinckney. *(to DR. PETRICOFF:)* Are you done with me now? Can I go?

DR. PETRICOFF. Wait a minute. What's the big hurry?

MR. PINCKNEY. Don't wanna waste my sight on a lousy hospital. Nursie and I could be at the movies right now.

HUGO. Thank God! Give thanks to God, Mr. Pinckney!

MR. PINCKNEY. *(to HUGO:)* Will you stop shouting at me? I never said I was deaf.

NURSE NOBLE. He can see, Doctor! He can see!

DR. PETRICOFF. And so can I, Miss Noble. I don't need you to tell me that. *(MR. PINCKNEY pinches NURSE NOBLE. She lets out a squeal and slaps him.)* Honestly, Mr. Pinckney! This is a medical center! *(to NURSE NOBLE:)* Show the man out, will you?

MR. PINCKNEY. *(nursing his slapped face)* She doesn't need to show me out! I can see for myself! Lousy patronizing doctors. All my life I been at the mercy of you jerks, and as far as I'm concerned you can shove it!

HUGO. Goodbye, Mr. Pinckney! Give thanks! *(MR. PINCKNEY Exits.)*

DR. PETRICOFF. I hope the next one shows a little more gratitude.

HUGO. He doesn't have to be grateful. He believed! He believed it would happen, and it did!

DR. PETRICOFF. Yes, well, this may be an isolated instance. Don't get your hopes up.

HUGO. He believed!

DR. PETRICOFF. Who says he did? He didn't sound like a believer to me. Hugo, my boy, we may be on to something, or we may not. I'd like to run a laboratory analysis on some of those pigeon droppings, if you don't mind. It's quite likely that there's some property in pigeon feces that we haven't discovered yet. If so...

Hugo. It's God's will.

Dr. Petricoff. Hey, do me a favor, will you? We want to play down that stuff. Let's not confuse the issue here, which is purely a medical phenomenon. Okay?

Hugo. But...

Dr. Petricoff. So if the press wants to call it a miracle, who can stop them? That's how they sell their papers. You know what a miracle is? It's a natural occurrence that hasn't yet been accounted for by scientific inquiry.

Hugo. No—you don't understand. It's God's will.

Dr. Petricoff. Okay, okay. It's God's will working through mysterious ways—and one of them is a medical phenomenon.

END OF SCENE 2

SCENE 3

An ORGAN chord sounds and we hear a T.V. ANNOUNCER'S voice.

Announcer. And now, live from St. Augustine, Florida, we bring you "God's Fan Club" with your companion in Christ, Harley Goodrich.

ACT II — ST. HUGO OF CENTRAL PARK

(The LIGHTS come up to reveal the set of the T.V. show. A CHOIR directed by HARLEY GOODRICH begins singing.)

CHOIR.
TIME TO LEND A HAND TO JESUS.
TIME TO HEAR IT FOR THE CAUSE.
GOD LOVES EVERYONE WHO SEES US,
SO LET'S GIVE HIM OUR APPLAUSE.

(Canned APPLAUSE. HARLEY GOODRICH turns to the camera.)

HARLEY GOODRICH. God's will be done! On behalf of our Lord Jesus Christ I thank you for the sweet sound of your applause. When I tell you I had a personal letter from God this past week, I know what you'll say. You'll say, "How is that possible, Harley?" Well, my friends, all things are possible to those who truly believe. I went to God's mailbox... *(He holds up his Bible.)* ...and I opened it up at random... *(emphasizing the miraculousness of this)* ...at random, my friends... and sure enough, there was a message in it just for me. It said, *(reading)* "Since the world began was it not heard that any man opened the eyes of one that was born blind. If the man were not of God, he could do nothing." Well, my friends, after I'd read these words I picked up the morning paper, and there, amid the horrifying reports of war, crime, pestilence and depravity that assault us daily, was the story of a Christian youth named Hugo DePew. It was an inspirational story, a story to renew one's faith at a time when the younger generation is wholly given over to the pursuit of drugs, drink, and demonic dancing. Most astonishing of all, it was a story that took place in that pit of moral squalor, the Sodom and Gomorrah of our day: New York City. It told of young Hugo, whose simple faith had endowed him with the ability to heal.

(LIGHTS dim on HARLEY as he continues to talk to the camera. They come up on HUGO.)

Hugo. I never should have gone on this T.V. show. I told them I didn't want to, but they said I had an obligation to spread the word of the Lord, and I was just too confused to know better.

(LIGHTS up on HARLEY.)

Harley Goodrich. And here he is, my friends: Hugo DePew.

(HUGO Enters and takes a seat beside HARLEY during canned APPLAUSE.)

Harley Goodrich. What a treat it is, in these godless times, to meet a young man like yourself.
Hugo. Thank you.
Harley Goodrich. I know you come from a Christian home.
Hugo. Sort of. I mean, we went to church.
Harley Goodrich. *(to the camera:)* You see, my friends? The family that prays together stays together.
Hugo. Well, they stay in Brooklyn. I stay in Central Park.

HARLEY GOODRICH. God's will be done! You know, here on "God's Fan Club" we like to say that if the young people of today came to know Christ at home and in the church, they'd walk in the paths of righteousness forever. Where was it, Hugo, that the knowledge and love of God first came upon you?

HUGO. In the reformatory.

HARLEY GOODRICH. Oh, yes? God's will be done. And can you remember the moment when your spiritual awakening began?

HUGO. I guess it was when God killed my psychiatrist.

HARLEY GOODRICH. When God what?

HUGO. Of course I'd been trying to get in touch with Him before that, but that's the first time I actually heard Him speak.

HARLEY GOODRICH. Speak? He spoke to you?

HUGO. Not to me, exactly. He said, "Who is this that darkens counsel by words without knowledge?"

HARLEY GOODRICH. *(to the camera:)* Well, there's no mistaking that voice, is there, my friends?

HUGO. At first I didn't understand what He meant, but it was pretty clear afterwards that He didn't think much of psychiatrists.

HARLEY GOODRICH. Amen to that! They're a heathen lot, Hugo. You might enjoy reading a pamphlet I wrote called "Don't Shrink Away from God."

HUGO. Well, okay.

HARLEY GOODRICH. This is really quite a fascinating story you have to share with us today, Hugo: the story of a young man who overcame the error of his ways and put his trust in the Lord. A story that sets a moral example for all of us, including yours truly, Harley Goodrich.

HUGO. Excuse me...

HARLEY GOODRICH. Yes?

HUGO. Well, you said I set an example, and the thing is, I don't know what it is. I'm real mixed up right now because even though I cured six blind people and five deaf ones at the medical center last week, there were, uh, complications.

HARLEY GOODRICH. Complications?

HUGO. That's what the doctor called them. He said not to talk about it, but I just have to. It happened again, just like with that reporter. Four of the people I touched got paralyzed.

HARLEY GOODRICH. Paralyzed?

HUGO. Uh-huh.

HARLEY GOODRICH. God's will be done.

HUGO. It's not even like the good people got healed and the bad ones didn't. I mean, I paralyzed a *nun*. It doesn't make any sense. I told the doctor I couldn't keep on trying to heal people when I was doing so much harm, but he wouldn't let me stop. They just kept coming and touching me, and because some people got cured, he said we had to keep going. But that can't be what God wants, can it?

HARLEY GOODRICH. Well now, that is a real question you've posed. A real *poser,* as my mama used to say when I asked her a Bible question she couldn't answer. Now let's just do what my mama had me do: let's look in God's mail box and see what's there.

HUGO. Huh?

ACT II   ST. HUGO OF CENTRAL PARK

HARLEY GOODRICH. *(holding up his Bible)* The word of the Lord! *(He opens it at random.)* Let's see what He has to say. Proverbs, Chapter 15, Verse 17.

HUGO. What does it say?

HARLEY GOODRICH. "Better is a dinner of herbs where love is, than a stalled ox and hatred therewith." Amen, Lord. Amen.

HUGO. Uh... Mr. Goodrich?

HARLEY GOODRICH. Yes?

HUGO. I don't know what that means.

HARLEY GOODRICH. Now look, Hugo. We're running short of time here, but I think the meaning is clear. It means, "Blessed is the man who believes in God."

HUGO. Well, I don't see how it...

HARLEY GOODRICH. *(breaking in)* "Love thy neighbor as thyself," Christ said.

HUGO. Yeah, I know, but...

HARLEY GOODRICH. Trust in the Lord!

HUGO. I do! It's just that...

HARLEY GOODRICH. *(cutting him off)* The old clock on the wall tells me we have to move on now. Thank you for being with us today and sharing your insights. *(He reaches out to shake HUGO'S hand.)*

HUGO. Well, you're welcome. But I don't understand. God doesn't want me to hurt people, does he?

HARLEY GOODRICH. *(writhing in pain as he grasps HUGO'S hand)* Aaaaaaaaaah! *(HARLEY freezes, paralyzed.)* Get him away from me! Get him away!

HUGO. Oh no! Mr. Goodrich! No!

(The "God's Fan Club" CHOIR Enters and hums a chorus of the

show's theme song as the LIGHTS fade out on HUGO and HARLEY.)

END OF SCENE 3

SCENE 4

HUGO appears in a SPOTLIGHT, speaking to the audience. The scene which follows covers events in his life from 1965 to 1967.

HUGO. This whole part of my life was like a long nightmare. I used to wake up screaming at night because I'd dreamed I touched somebody. All I wanted was to keep away from people but everybody was after me to do something. Like my parents, for example.

(The LIGHTS come up to reveal MR. and MRS. DEPEW, who are speaking to HUGO.)

MRS. DEPEW. Honey, I know you feel bad about those people and all, but it's just not your fault. It's like the doctor says: at this point, your responsibility is to help medical research in any way you can.

MR. DEPEW. That's right. This idea about the Hugo DePew Foundation is what I think you oughta latch onto. It'd set you up for life.

(The LIGHTS come up on DR. PETRICOFF, also speaking to HUGO.)

DR. PETRICOFF. You see, Hugo, I was thinking how we might use these...as-yet-unaccountable properties of yours...to further the cause of medicine throughout the world.

HUGO. How?

DR. PETRICOFF. Well, you know, getting cured is a big thing in a lot of people's lives, and people don't usually expect to get something for nothing. They value a thing more, y'know, if they have to pay for it. It's a basic principle of medicine.

MR. DEPEW. He's right, Hugo. It is.

DR. PETRICOFF. What I was thinking was, if there were a nominal charge, part of that money could go into medical research and help cure other diseases. Of course we wouldn't charge the people who got...

MRS. DEPEW. We understand, Doctor.

DR. PETRICOFF. Anything you can't handle, y'see, we fund out of the profits.

MR. DEPEW. So even more people would be helped, right?

DR. PETRICOFF. That's it. We'd call it the Hugo DePew Foundation, and you'd get to have an office and a secretary...

MR. DEPEW. And a dictaphone.

HUGO. No! Can't you see? I can't!

MRS. DEPEW. Honey, anybody can use a dictaphone. It's easy.

HUGO. Mama...

MRS. DEPEW. You're famous, Hugo. You need a secretary just to handle the fan mail.

DR. PETRICOFF. Of course, part of the profits'll go to the pigeons, too. Whadda they like—bread?

HUGO. Yeah, they like bread.

DR. PETRICOFF. Well, how d'ya think cake would sound to them?

HUGO. Cake? But I don't...

DR. PETRICOFF. Cake, their own park—you name it.

MRS. DEPEW. The DePew Pigeon Park!

DR. PETRICOFF. You could afford to lobby for the rights of pigeons everywhere. Put an end to injustice.

MR. DEPEW. Your name in the papers, Hugo: The Pigeons' Pal!

DR. PETRICOFF. An end to affliction! No more disease!

MR. DEPEW. You can't keep a thing like this under wraps, Hugo.

DR. PETRICOFF. It's not Christian.

HUGO. What?

MRS. DEPEW. You got a talent, baby. Use it!

MR. DEPEW. Make something of yourself!

DR. PETRICOFF. The way I see it, you don't have any choice. A gift like yours isn't something you can futz around with, Hugo; it belongs to the world.

(MR. and MRS. DEPEW and DR. PETRICOFF, who are all making gestures of appeal toward HUGO, suddenly freeze in position, and the LIGHTS dim on all three. HUGO speaks to them while they remain frozen.)

ACT II ST. HUGO OF CENTRAL PARK 73

HUGO. I can't! I can't! Doesn't anybody understand? I can't go on hurting *some* people in order help other people. I can't!

(The LIGHTS on MR. and MRS. DEPEW return to normal intensity, and they are reanimated. DR. PETRICOFF remains frozen in HALF-LIGHT.)

MR. DEPEW. What about Mr. Porter?
MRS. DEPEW. Surely you see the sense of that, Hugo.
MR. DEPEW. All he wants you to do is endorse his line of little Hugo dolls.
MRS. DEPEW. They'll make money, baby—for the hungry kids in India. Don't you want to help people?
MR. DEPEW. We're committed, Hugo. It's a commitment. I told him to go ahead. We only get 20 per cent. Porter gets 50, but the rest goes to a good cause. So what's wrong with that?
MRS. DEPEW. He just wants you... Hugo, are you listening to me? He wants you to heal somebody. That's not too much to ask, is it?

(The LIGHTS come up on PERRY PORTER, the maker of the HUGO dolls.)

MR. PORTER. Look, Hugo. You're in business; I'm in business. Your business is healing people; mine's making dolls. But the thing is, nobody's buying. And the reason ain't too hard to guess. Nobody's buying the Hugo number because you're on the skids. Now, we got a warehouse on Long Island full of eighty-five thousand little Hugos, and we might as well have eighty-five thousand little Hitlers for all the good it's doin' us. People don't want 'em. Hell, a lot of people are even afraid to touch 'em. Y' know why? I'll tell you why. 'Cause the last thing they saw you do was zap Harley Goodrich on "God's Fan Club." You haven't actually healed anybody in eleven months. And that article in the National Enquirer about how you raped that hooker didn't help.

Mrs. Depew. He did not rape any hooker.

Mr. Porter. That's what it said, lady. Who wants a little rapist doll? I'll tell you who: nobody. So what I say is, get off your ass and do something. Heal somebody big. Is Helen Keller still alive? Well, if she is, give her a call. But please God, Hugo, don't zap her. One more zap and you're all washed up. Hugo? You listening to me?

Hugo. I feel sick.

Mr. Porter. Terrific. You feel sick, and I'm losing a hundred grand. Well, if you feel sick, why the hell don't you heal yourself? What'd ya do? Zap yourself?

Mr. Depew. Now, wait a minute!

Hugo. Get out of here! Get out of here right now or I'm gonna touch you!

Mr. Depew. Hugo! Don't!

Mr. Porter. What's got into you?

Hugo. I mean it. I'm gonna touch you, and you won't be healed, either.

Mr. Depew. Hugo, put down that hand!

Mr. Porter. I'm going, I'm going. But just remember this, Mr. Holy Hugo: you ain't got it in ya to heal anybody anymore. Y'know what they call you where I live? They

ACT II   ST. HUGO OF CENTRAL PARK

call you The Zapper. Ladies and gentleman, step right up and get zapped by the one-and-only Zapper! So long, Zapper. See ya in the funny papers.

(MR. PORTER is frozen in an angry gesture; his SPOTLIGHT dims.)

MRS. DEPEW. Hugo?
HUGO. Yeah, Mama?
MRS. DEPEW. What do you want to do, honey? You can't just turn your back on everything.
HUGO. Why not?
MR. DEPEW. Don't you want things? You can have 'em, Hugo.
MRS. DEPEW. You can do great things, honey.
HUGO. Mama—Dad. I don't want to *have* anything. I don't even want to *do* anything anymore. I just want to be.
MRS. DEPEW. What does that mean? Edgar, do you know what that means?
HUGO. Everybody tells me to do this or do that—that the good thing to do is to make money for starving children or to help put an end to disease. And those *are* good things, I know it. It's just that... Everybody told me I was a saint. Well, I don't know what that means. They said it was so great that I wasn't into all the things that gave other people pleasure, but they didn't understand.
MRS. DEPEW. Understand what?
HUGO. That I *had* the greatest pleasure in the world.

Mrs. Depew. What was that, baby?

Hugo. God, Mama. Trying to be worthy of God.

Mrs. Depew. You talk to him, Edgar. I just can't talk to him when he's like this.

Mr. Depew. You think I can? What does he want, that's what I want to know. What does he want? This time last year he was a big success, now he's screwing it up. Hugo, what is it you *want?*

Hugo. I want... to be good.

Mr. Depew. Damn it, Hugo, I'm your father. Can't you give me a straight answer? Everybody wants to be good. But you have to be pretty dumb to let that stand in the way of accomplishing things.

Mrs. Depew. *(to HUGO:)* Listen to him, baby.

Mr. Depew. Now, the way I see it, maybe God slipped up a little when he gave you this gift. Nobody's perfect, right?

Mrs. Depew. I talked to a priest about it, and he said if you confessed right after you paralyzed people, God wouldn't mind a bit.

Mr. Depew. You see? I mean, if it's okay upstairs...

Hugo. Get away from me! Get away! I didn't ask to be the way I am, and I don't know why God made me this way, but *He* knows.

Mr. Depew. Hugo, be reasonable. There's money at stake here.

Hugo. Damn you!

Mrs. Depew. Hugo!

Hugo. Damn you both! May the Lord God damn you both to hell!

ST. HUGO OF CENTRAL PARK

(The LIGHTS go out on MR. and MRS. DEPEW. HUGO speaks to the audience.)

HUGO. I wish I hadn't had to say what I said to my parents, but I did. One thing I learned as I got older was that even the people who love you most in the world would rather have you go against your beliefs than go against *them*. So I just ran away from everybody and kept on running. I didn't know where I was going, and I didn't care. I remember running through the streets, screaming at people to get away from me: anybody, everybody— just get away! It was like I *had* to scream, I had to keep moving. Whenever I'd slow down I'd start thinking, God hates me! He hates me! He was the only one who ever really understood, but now He hates me for what I did— going along with all those people who wanted me to use my powers in the wrong way. Sometimes I'd fall asleep in an alley or a doorway or someplace, but I wouldn't sleep for long. I couldn't. As soon as I woke up I'd have to start running again, like I was some kind of rat in a maze and there was no way out—just city streets forever. I was so blinded by thinking about myself all the time that I didn't know where I was or what I was doing. And then one day when I woke up I was in the park again, and it came to me all of a sudden that I'd forgotten what I was meant to do. I was supposed to be taking care of the pigeons, not thinking about myself. Now, God could have told me that, but He didn't. He waited for me to figure it out on my own. I was in this big meadow, and suddenly it happened just like before: all these pigeons came at me, and I could see the sun on their wings and on their necks—and everywhere I looked it was like a rainbow, a rainbow!

(FADE OUT)

END OF SCENE 4

SCENE 5

The LIGHTS come up on JILL GERARD, the movie-land gossip reporter, speaking to a television camera. The year is 1968.

JILL GERARD. Hello out there! This is Jill Gerard, reporting from Hollywood, where the big news tonight is that Howard Hester wants Hugo DePew, the young man who made such a big splash as a miracle healer a few years ago, to appear as Jesus Christ in his new movie "That Boy From Bethlehem." Howard's problem at the moment is that he can't get in touch with young Hugo to give him the good news. Seems that Hugo has disappeared! His parents, who were the last people to see him since late February, say they don't know where he is. If you're watching, Hugo, this is it! Hollywood calls, and who can turn down someone like Howard Hester?

(The LIGHTS go out on JILL GERARD. PERRY PORTER appears in a SPOTLIGHT.)

MR. PORTER. This is it! I'm saved! We make little robes for the dolls, see, and we call them "That Boy." Suddenly we got an empty warehouse on Long Island and three hundred grand in the bank! Suddenly we ain't going bankrupt at all! It's perfect. Perfect! I could kiss Howard Hester's foot! But where the hell's Hugo?

(The LIGHTS come up on DR. PETRICOFF, who speaks to MR. PORTER.)

DR. PETRICOFF. Hollywood? It's ridiculous. Hugo's no actor.
MR. PORTER. So who is? Look, at this point I'll bet he can act a hell of a lot better than he can heal.

(The LIGHTS dim on MR. PORTER and DR. PETRICOFF and come up on MR. and MRS. DEPEW.)

MRS. DEPEW. I can't believe it! Hugo in the movies!
MR. DEPEW. I always told you he'd come through.
MRS. DEPEW. Who'll they get to play his mother?
MR. DEPEW. Who?
MRS. DEPEW. You know: Mary.
MR. DEPEW. How do I know?
MRS. DEPEW. Wouldn't it be funny if...
MR. DEPEW. If what?
MRS. DEPEW. Well, if...
MR. DEPEW. What?
MRS. DEPEW. Well, they wouldn't. But just think! The movies! Honestly, Edgar, it's too good to be true!

(The LIGHTS go out on MR. and MRS. DEPEW, MR. PORTER, and DR. PETRICOFF, and a SOLOIST appears.)

SOLOIST.
SAINT HUGO HEARD TWO VOICES:
THE FIRST WAS FROM ON HIGH.
THE SECOND CAME FROM HOLLYWOOD.
HE SAID HE'D RATHER DIE.

(CROSS-FADE on SOLOIST. The LIGHTS come up on RON BLODGETT, a T.V. reporter, interviewing HUGO in Central Park as DR. PETRICOFF looks on. HUGO is holding a pigeon.)

RON BLODGETT. This is Ron Blodgett of Channel 8 News in Central Park with Hugo DePew, the young man who surprised the nation by turning down the lead role in Howard Hester's new multi-million dollar epic about the life of Christ.
DR. PETRICOFF. He didn't turn it down. He's thinking it over.
RON BLODGETT. And we also have with us Dr. Oscar Petricoff, Hugo's personal physician.
HUGO. He isn't. I don't even know what he's doing here.
DR. PETRICOFF. Now, Hugo...
HUGO. *(holding up the pigeon)* See? His name is Ozzie.
RON BLODGETT. Oh yes?
HUGO. He sprained his wing two days ago, but you wouldn't know it now, would you?

ACT II ST. HUGO OF CENTRAL PARK 81

Ron Blodgett. Looks fine to me.

Hugo. Ever since Rosalinda died he's been accident-prone. They weren't always happy together, but since her death... *(to the pigeon:)* Well, you just need extra attention, don't you?

Ron Blodgett. Uh... I'd like to ask a few questions.

Hugo. Talk a little louder, then. He's kinda deaf.

Ron Blodgett. No—I mean, I'd like to ask *you* some questions. About your reason for not wanting to appear in "That Boy from Bethlemen."

Dr. Petricoff. He's a little disturbed, Mr. Blodgett. He...

Hugo. I'm not disturbed, and I don't want to talk about any movie.

Ron Blodgett. Well, Hugo, there's an audience out there who'd like to know why you decided against it. If you could just say a few words...

Hugo. Why do they want to know? I won't even *be* here.

Ron Blodgett. What?

Dr. Petricoff. He means he's considering it.

Ron Blodgett. What do you mean, you won't even be here? What will you be doing?

Hugo. Dying.

Ron Blodgett. Dying! What makes you think you're going to die, Hugo?

Dr. Petricoff. Mr. Blodgett, I think...

Ron Blodgett. *(to DR. PETRICOFF:)* Excuse me. *(to HUGO:)* Answer the question, son.

Dr. Petricoff. This is brutal.

Hugo. Because God told me I was going to die.

Ron Blodgett. God told you. Did he tell you when? *(HUGO nods.)* Could you tell us, then?

Dr. Petricoff. Hugo!

Hugo. It's all right. I don't care if people know.

Dr. Petricoff. Well, *I* care.

Hugo. That's because you think I'm crazy, but I'm not. I'm gonna die on March 21st.

Ron Blodgett. March 21st.

Hugo. At 7:30 p.m.

Dr. Petricoff. *(to BLODGETT:)* Now are you satisfied? He's suffering from severe emotional distress, and if you have any conscience at all, you won't continue this.

Ron Blodgett. Please, Doctor. *(to HUGO:)* How did He tell you?

Hugo. He spoke to me. He said I was going to die, and I should stay here and help the pigeons until the time comes.

Dr. Petricoff. Hugo! *(to the camera:)* He isn't even sick!

Hugo. That's what He told me. And even if I wasn't going to die, I shouldn't be making movies. I should be doing what I *can* do, which is to take care of the birds.

Dr. Petricoff. *(to BLODGETT:)* You see? This is getting us nowhere. Hugo doesn't choose to make the movie. That's that.

Ron Blodgett. Why March 21st?

Hugo. I don't know.

Ron Blodgett. How are you going to die?

Hugo. I don't know that, either.

Dr. Petricoff. *(to BLODGETT:)* Please! Can't you leave him alone?

RON BLODGETT. Well, how do you feel about dying, Hugo?

HUGO. Wonderful! He wants me. It's wonderful!

DR. PETRICOFF. Hugo, please!

RON BLODGETT. *(to HUGO:)* Is there anything you want to say to the people who are watching?

HUGO. Just that it's the most wonderful thing that ever happened to me, and I'm really happy. I'm gonna be with God, and I won't have to worry about hurting people anymore. Oh, and if there's anybody out there watching who got hurt by me, I just wanna say: forgive me.

DR. PETRICOFF. Thank you, Mr. Blodgett. That will be all. Hugo, come on.

RON BLODGETT. But...!

DR. PETRICOFF. I refuse to allow him to answer any more questions. Hugo!

RON BLODGETT. Wait a minute! What did God look like?

HUGO. I didn't see Him; I just heard Him.

DR. PETRICOFF. Good day, Mr. Blodgett! Come along, Hugo. *(as he drags him out)* Hugo! Hugo, come on.

END OF SCENE 5

SCENE 6

It is March 21, 1968, shortly before 7:30 p.m. The setting is Sheep Meadow in Central Park. HUGO Enters and sits down;

throughout the scene he will remain seated, unaware of everything going on around him. During the following song a crowd assembles to wait for the announced moment of death, and the stage is set as they bring on television equipment, picnic baskets, pennants, etc.—all the paraphernalia necessary for the big event.

CROWD.
NOW THE MOMENT WE'VE BEEN WAITING FOR.
NOW THE JUDGEMENT DAY IS NIGH.
SHOW THE PEOPLE WHAT THEY'RE WAITING FOR:
SHOW THE DOUBTERS HOW YOU DIE.

NOW THE MOMENT WE'VE BEEN WAITING FOR.
NOW YOU DRAW YOUR FINAL BREATH.
GIVE THE PEOPLE WHAT THEY'RE PAYING FOR:
GIVE US ALL A TASTE OF DEATH.

ALL YOUR LIFE'S A HOLY MYSTERY.
ALL YOUR LESSONS WILL LIVE ON.
WE WILL SEE YOU LIVE IN HISTORY.
WE'LL ADORE YOU WHEN YOU'RE GONE.

(MUSIC continues under. A HAWKER walks by with a load of dolls.)

HAWKER. Get your Hugo dolls! Buy a souvenir for the

kids! Get your Hugo dolls!

(PERRY PORTER appears from the crowd.)

MR. PORTER. *(to HAWKER:)* How're they selling?

HAWKER. Real slow. Everybody wants to wait until after, ya know what I mean? Can't blame 'em, either. I'd feel real stupid if I paid eight bucks for a Hugo doll and then nothin' happened.

MR. PORTER. How many ya sell?

HAWKER. Three.

MR. PORTER. Three?

HAWKER. Look, it ain't easy. I get all kinds. I mean like a lotta people are offended by me bein' here.

MR. PORTER. Yeah?

HAWKER. You'd be surprised. But if he pulls it off, I'll go clean in a coupla minutes. That's the way it is. If he pulls it off, I could sell the whole truckload. If not—well, you're gonna hafta ditch a lotta dolls.

(The CROWD begins singing again. As they sing RON BLODGETT consults with his camera crew. JILL GERARD joins him.)

CROWD.	RON BLODGETT. *(ad lib)* Testing, testing, one-two-three. Are the cameras ready to roll? How do I look? Okay? Let's tape the intro and then go right into the rest. What? We got time. Get those girls
PEOPLE WANT TO SEE SOME EVIDENCE.	
PEOPLE WANT TO SEE A SHOW.	
NOW'S THE TIME TO GIVE THE EVIDENCE.	
NOW'S THE TIME FOR YOU TO GO.	

NOW THE MOMENT WE'VE BEEN WAITING FOR.
NOW THE JUDGEMENT DAY IS NIGH.
SHOW THE PEOPLE WHAT THEY'RE WAITING FOR:
SHOW THE DOUBTERS HOW YOU DIE.

NOW THE MOMENT WE'VE BEEN PRAYING FOR:
NOW YOU DRAW YOUR FINAL BREATH.
GIVE THE PEOPLE WHAT THEY'RE PAYING FOR:
GIVE US ALL
GIVE US ALL A TASTE
GIVE US ALL A TASTE OF...

out of the way, will you? Hey, Jerry—zoom in on Hugo when I go like this. Got it? Okay, any time. Peter Piper picked a peck of pickled peppers. Here we go...

RON BLODGETT. Good evening. This is Ron Blodgett, your roving reporter for Channel 8 News, standing by with...

JILL GERARD. Jill Gerard!

RON BLODGETT. We're here tonight in Central Park's Sheep Meadow to witness what many people think will be a truly remarkable event: the death of Hugo DePew, the miracle healer, who claims he received word from God that he was to die at 7:30 p.m.

JILL GERARD. That's 6:30 Central Time. 4:30 for all of you out there in God's country, which is what I call the West coast.

RON BLODGETT. Right, Jill. DePew is here now—

looking remarkably fit, I must say, for a young man who claims he only has four more minutes to live. Tension has been mounting all evening, as the more than... How many people would you say are here, Jill?

JILL GERARD. Well, Ron, I'd say there are more than 50,000 people here tonight. And they seem to come from all walks of life. There's the middle-aged...

RON BLODGETT. Thank you, Jill. How would you describe what Hugo is wearing tonight?

JILL GERARD. Well, it's his usual mode of dress, and I guess that's pretty familiar to most people. There's the burlap smock covered with pigeon droppings...

(Upstage, a couple of CHEERLEADERS are performing for the crowd. Their cheer interrupts JILL's account.)

CHEERLEADERS.
One, two, three-four-five!
We love you, Hugo, dead or alive!
Six, seven, eight-nine-ten!
We think you're a prince among men!
Yay, Hugo!

JILL GERARD. Now that's what I call team spirit, Ron.

RON BLODGETT. You said it, Jill. We just have time here for a word from our special commentator tonight, Mr. Harley Goodrich. Harley?

(HARLEY GOODRICH comes on in a walker.)

HARLEY GOODRICH. God's will be done, Ron.

RON BLODGETT. Same to you, Harley. Now, I know you've had close contact with young Hugo DePew.

HARLEY GOODRICH. I don't hold it against him! Our Lord Jesus Christ said, "He that is without sin among you, let him cast a first stone." This deranged boy from a reformatory came on my show and afflicted me with an incurable paralysis, but I tell you, my friends, I don't hold it against him.

RON BLODGETT. Well, I see. And how do you feel about his death tonight?

HARLEY GOODRICH. Good! I feel good!

RON BLODGETT. Yes, but do you think it will happen?

HARLEY GOODRICH. Ron, I can only say: God's will be done.

RON BLODGETT. Brave words, Harley. Well, people seem to be starting the countdown with the help of the giant clock that was donated by the Schaefer Brewing Company. Two minutes to go, and I want to try to ask Hugo a few questions. *(going over to HUGO)* Hugo? Hugo? It's Ron Blodgett from Channel 8. I wanted to ask you what you'll do if you don't die tonight. Will you reconsider going into the movies, or will you go back to healing pigeons? Hugo? Well, he doesn't seem to be saying anything to anyone at the moment. No last words? Jill, do you want to try?

JILL GERARD. Hugo, it's Jill Gerard. I was wondering how it feels to be facing death. Could you say a few words about that? You have a little more than a minute now, and I was hoping that you'd say something sort of inspiring. Is your whole life flashing before you, Hugo? I'm afraid he won't talk, Ron.

Ron Blodgett. Well, it's the chance of a lifetime, but I guess there's nothing he wants to say. It's sort of hard to think how he's gonna die, you know, since he isn't sick or anything. Does he look sick to you, Jill?

Jill Gerard. No, he doesn't, Ron.

Ron Blodgett. Harley?

Harley Goodrich. He always looked sick to me, Ron.

Ron Blodgett. Wait a minute! Here it comes: the big one. We're approaching the last ten seconds. Let's count along with them, Jill.

Jill, Blodgett & Crowd. 10, 9, 8, 7, 6, 5, 4, 3, 2, 1 — ZERO!

Ron Blodgett. What happened?

Jill Gerard. Nothing, Ron. It's 7:30 p.m. and nothing happened.

Ron Blodgett. Well, I guess Hugo will...

(Suddenly a SHOT rings out and HUGO falls over, dead. The CROWD starts running around madly.)

Jill Gerard. What was that?

Ron Blodgett. A shot! Somebody shot him! Somebody shot him! Hugo DePew has been shot, at exactly 7:30 and ten seconds! The crowd is running for cover, and... Jill? Jill, where are you?

(JILL GERARD has run for cover. BLODGETT goes toward HUGO's body. FLASHBULBS go off.)

RON BLODGETT. Oh my God, he's all covered with blood! This is Ron Blodgett, reporting from Sheep Meadow, where Hugo DePew has been shot!

HAWKER. Hugo dolls! Get your Hugo dolls! Buy a souvenir for the kids!

(BLACKOUT.)

SCENE 7

The LIGHTS come up on a television talk show with hosts RON BLODGETT and JILL GERARD and guests DR. PETRICOFF and MRS. DEPEW. It is October, 1968.

RON BLODGETT. There's nothing to be nervous about, Mrs. DePew; we'll just chat normally for the camera, just the way we are now. All right? *(into the camera:)* Good evening. We're here tonight with the mother of Hugo DePew, the young man whose spectacular death six months ago attracted world-wide attention. We'll also be chatting with Dr. Oscar Petricoff, Hugo's close friend and personal physician. I'd like to begin with you, Mrs. DePew. We know now that your son was shot by Perry Porter, the doll manufacturer. And yet there seems to be a great cult in this country which maintains that he was actually struck down by God at the appointed time. How would you explain the seeming contradiction?

MRS. DEPEW. I don't think there *is* a contradiction.

Hugo said that God had told him he was going to die at 7:30 p.m. on March 21st, and he *did* die at 7:30 p.m. God knew, apparently, that Mr. Porter was going to shoot him.

JILL GERARD. Mrs. DePew: Porter himself said that he shot your son because he was afraid that otherwise he wouldn't die. He wanted to sell those shoddy dolls of his.

MRS. DEPEW. I know that. And I know, too, that Hugo had been told by God that he was going to die. At the time I didn't know what to believe, but now I can see it was true. It's taken me many long months to straighten it all out in my mind, but now I understand that my son Hugo was a holy martyr.

DR. PETRICOFF. Now, Mrs. DePew...

MRS. DEPEW. Don't try to reason with me, Doctor. I know what I know, and there are a great many people who agree with me. The reason I came on this show at all was to let people know that Hugo's mother believes in her son—and so does his father, for that matter (Edgar wanted to come, he really did.)—and to tell them that Hugo DePew was truly a saint. You may not believe it, but we do.

RON BLODGETT. What do you believe, Doctor?

DR. PETRICOFF. I believe Hugo DePew was the most remarkable individual I ever met.

MRS. DEPEW. Well, it comes to the same thing, doesn't it?

DR. PETRICOFF. No. You believe he was a man of God, and I don't believe in God at all.

RON BLODGETT. Excuse me...

MRS. DEPEW. You don't believe in God? Well, how did he do it, then?

RON BLODGETT. Excuse me, please...

MRS. DEPEW. How did he do all those things? Of course it was God!

RON BLODGETT. Mrs. DePew—Doctor. I hate to break off this fascinating discussion you're having, but I'm afraid we have to pause, as usual, for the commercial.

(The LIGHTS begin to fade on the talk show as MRS. DEPEW and DR. PETRICOFF continue to argue. A SOLOIST Enters, singing. Dialogue fades out as the song ends.)

MRS. DEPEW. *(ignoring BLODGETT)* If it wasn't God, what was it?

DR. PETRICOFF. We don't know yet.

MRS. DEPEW. Don't know yet? What kind of an answer is that?

DR. PETRICOFF. A scientific one.

MRS. DEPEW. Oh, don't give me that.

DR. PETRICOFF. It's a damn sight better than calling that kid a holy martyr. He was a sick kid, that's what he was.

SOLOIST.
SAINT HUGO WAS A MARTYR;
HE DIED FOR YOU AND ME.
HIS LIFE WAS BRIEF BUT BEAUTIFUL.
HIS DEATH WAS ON T.V.

SAINT HUGO, OH, SAINT HUGO,
WHY WILL WE NEVER LEARN?
SAINTS ARE BORN TO LEAD THE WAY
AND NEVER TO RETURN.

MRS. DEPEW. Sick? What do you mean, sick? Hugo was a saint, and if you think being a saint means being sick, then God help you.

DR. PETRICOFF. There's just no talking to you people. "My son Hugo was a holy martyr." Well, you can believe what you want to believe, and I'll believe the truth.

MRS. DEPEW. I pity you, that's all I can say. I won't say another word.

DR. PETRICOFF. Good! I'm sick to death of this whole argument.

MRS. DEPEW. You're sick of it? What do you think I am?

(BLACKOUT on everyone; MUSIC continues under. HUGO appears in a SPOTLIGHT, speaking to the audience.)

HUGO. I thought maybe if I showed you what my whole life was like, I might understand it better, and find out why people thought I was so unusual. But I still don't really understand. What I know now is what I knew when I was just a kid: that there was something inside of me that made me want to be better than I was. As I got older, I had to try harder and harder to hold onto it, because I couldn't really *explain* it to anyone—and besides, people didn't want to hear about it. It was like they didn't want to be reminded that they ever felt that way, too. Well, now people keep praying to me for advice all the time, because they think I set some kind of example. I tell them to listen to the voice of God inside themselves and keep trying to be good in their own way; but usually when I tell them that, I never hear from them again. So now I just say: God bless you, everybody! God bless you, and keep you, and make His face to shine upon you. May God lift up his countenance upon you, and give you peace, now and forevermore.

(The LIGHT goes out.)

THE END

PROPERTY PLOT

ACT I, SCENE 1
2 cantaloupes (foam rubber)
Desk blotter
Clipboard and pencil for Dr. Kitchener
Papers and forms
Cantaloupe pieces

ACT I, SCENE 2
Desk blotter
Papers and forms
Clipboard and pencil for Dr. Kitchener

ACT I, SCENE 3
Book for Hugo
Magazine for Mrs. DePew

ACT I, SCENE 4
Hairbrush for Susie

ACT I, SCENE 5
Nail file for Mrs. DePew

ACT I, SCENE 6
Pigeon for Hugo
Purse and handkerchief for Martha
Popsicle sticks for Hugo
Camera and dark glasses for Elroy

ACT II, SCENE 1
Four note pads and pencils for reporters

ACT II, SCENE 2
Folder and pen for Dr. Petricoff

ACT II, SCENE 3
Bible for Harley Goodrich

ACT II, SCENE 5
Two microphones for Jill Gerard and Ron Blodgett
Pigeon for Hugo

ACT II, SCENE 6
Vendor tray with Hugo dolls for Hawker
Two microphones with cords for Jill and Ron
Walker for Harley
Gun with blanks (offstage)
Flash camera

COSTUME PLOT

ACT I

SCENE 1
MR. MUNCY:
White shirt
Dark blue tie with small yellow stripe
2 piece blue suit
Black belt
Black socks and black loafers

MRS. DEPEW:
2 piece turquoise knit outfit
Beige knit top
Beige patent leather pumps
Beige pill box hat
Beige gloves
Beige purse
Turquoise beads
Gold earrings and watch
Pantyhose and slip

HUGO:
Clean hair shirt (underdressed)
Beige shirt
Belt
Grey socks and penny loafers
Grey cotton pants

SCENE 2
DR. KITCHENER:
Dark brown wig
2 piece magenta suit
Navy heels and pantyhose
Brooch

MR. MUNCY:
Takes off suit jacket and loosens tie.

HUGO:
Same as Scene 1

CHOIR:
Red choir robes
White surplices

SCENE 3
MRS. DEPEW:
Tan housedress with self belt
Pantyhose and slip
Black mesh heels
Gold watch and earrings
Wig

HUGO:
Removes beige shirt.

MR. DEPEW:
White shirt
Navy trousers with small stripe

Black socks and black wing tips
Black belt and suspenders
Maroon cardigan

SCENE 4
CHOIR:
Same as Scene 3

SUSIE:
Beige silk slip
Blue cocktail dress
Black heels with bow
Bra
Gold earrings

HUGO:
Adds beige windbreaker.

SCENE 5
CHOIR:
Same as Scene 4

MR. DEPEW:
White shirt
Grey cardigan
Navy trousers with belt and suspenders
Black socks and black wing tips

MRS. DEPEW:
Royal blue dress with self belt
Slip and pantyhose

Black mesh heels
Gold brooch
Gold earrings and watch
Gold bead necklace
Wig

SCENE 6
HUGO:
Dirty hair shirt
Dark grey twill pants with belt
Grey socks
Dirty sneakers

JUDY:
Wig
2 piece green pantsuit
Brown striped blouse
Brown suede shoes

MARTHA:
Grey wig
Green floral silk dress
Pantyhose
Brown purse
Brown pumps
Gold earrings and ring

ELROY:
Blue jeans
Blue jean jacket
Gold knit shirt

Sunglasses
Black socks and black mesh shoes

JOHN:
White shirt
Cufflinks
Red tie
3 piece navy blue wool suit
Black belt
Black socks and black shoes
Navy blue fedora

POLICEMAN:
Blue shirt
Blue tie
Policeman's uniform
Policeman's belt
Policeman's hat and badges
Black socks and black shoes

ACT II

SCENE 1
REPORTER #1:
Navy trenchcoat
Brown fedora
Black socks and black shoes
(underdressed Harley)

REPORTER #2:
Grey fedora
Beige trenchcoat and belt

Black pumps
Scarf
(underdressed Nurse Noble)

REPORTER #3:
Navy fedora
Beige trenchcoat
Black socks and black shoes
(underdressed Dr. Petricoff)

REPORTER #4:
Green fedora
Green trenchcoat
Black socks and shoes
(underdressed Mr. Pinckney)

HUGO:
Same as Act I, Scene 6

SCENE 2
DR. PETRICOFF:
White shirt with cufflinks
Green striped tie
3 piece green suit
Black belt
Black socks and black shoes
Glasses

MR. PINCKNEY:
Grey wig
Hat

Tan striped shirt
Gold sweater vest
Black striped pants
Suspenders
Grey tweed jacket
Black knit scarf
Dark blue overcoat
Black socks and black mesh shoes

NURSE NOBLE:
Blonde wig and hairband
White uniform
Bra and pantyhose
Beige shoes

HUGO:
Same

SCENE 4
HUGO:
Same

MR. DEPEW:
White shirt
Blue bowtie
Maroon sweater
Navy pants with black belt and suspenders
Black socks and black wing tips

MRS. DEPEW:
2 piece striped tan dress

Pantyhose and slip
Wig
Pearls and pearl earrings
Beige pumps
Watch

DR. PETRICOFF:
Same as Scene 2

PERRY PORTER:
Green overcoat
Brown fedora
Brown knit muffler

SCENE 5
JILL:
Green/black Chanel style suit
Black pumps
Small pearl earrings
Pearl necklaces and chains
Beige blouse with ruffles

MR. DEPEW:
Same as Scene 4

MRS. DEPEW:
Same as Scene 4

HUGO:
Same

DR. PETRICOFF:
White shirt with cufflinks
2 piece tan suit
Brown tie
Glasses
Brown shoes and socks

RON:
White shirt
2 piece greyish green suit
Greyish green leather gloves
Green overcoat
Black belt
Grey scarf
Black socks and black loafers

HUGO:
Same

DR. PETRICOFF:
Adds overcoat with fur collar.

SCENE 6
HUGO:
Same

JILL:
Beige blouse
2 piece beige/brown checked suit
Gold necklace and gold earrings
Pantyhose

Beige knit gloves
Beige overcoat
Brown spectators

RON:
Same as Scene 5

MRS. DEPEW:
Black overcoat with fur collar
Black pumps
Black purse
Black gloves
Pantyhose
Wig with black scarf
Pearl earrings and necklace
Black velvet hat
2 piece black suit
Circle pin

HARLEY:
Adds gold colored overcoat and checked scarf.

PERRY PORTER:
Adds leather gloves.

SPECTATOR (DR. PETRICOFF):
Removes overcoat.
Adds navy blue wool overcoat.
Navy fedora
Red scarf
Black leather gloves
(underdressed Dr. P.)

SPECTATOR (NURSE NOBLE):
Adds black knit scarf.
Red and black overcoat
Black pumps

HAWKER:
Adds black leather gloves.
Tan wool overcoat
Grey fedora
Yellow muffler

SCENE 7
HUGO:
Removes hair shirt and adds beige shirt.

RON:
Removes gloves, scarf and overcoat.

JILL:
Removes overcoat, gloves, jacket.

DR. PETRICOFF:
Removes fedora, scarf, overcoat, gloves.

CHOIR:
Red choir robes
White surplices

MRS. DEPEW:
Removes coat, gloves, scarf, purse.

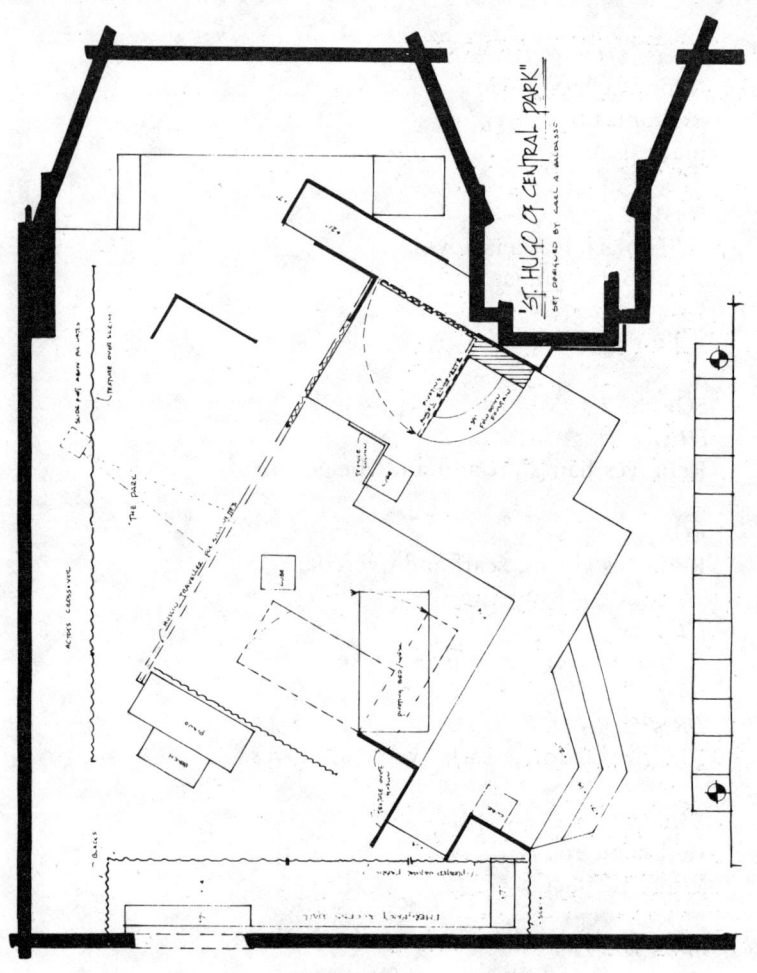

Other Publications for Your Interest

COMING ATTRACTIONS
(ADVANCED GROUPS—COMEDY WITH MUSIC)

By TED TALLY, music by JACK FELDMAN, lyrics by BRUCE SUSSMAN and FELDMAN

5 men, 2 women—Unit Set

Lonnie Wayne Burke has the requisite viciousness to be a media celebrity—but he lacks vision. When we meet him, he is holding only four people hostage in a laundromat. There aren't any cops much less reporters around, because they're across town where some guy is holding 50 hostages. But, a talent agent named Manny sees possibilities in Lonnie Wayne. He devises a criminal persona for him by dressing him in a skeleton costume and sending him door-to-door, murdering people as "The Hallowe'en Killer". He is captured, and becomes an instant celebrity, performing on TV shows. When his fame starts to wane, he crashes the Miss America Pageant disguised as Miss Wyoming to kill Miss America on camera. However, he falls in love with her, and this eventually leads to his downfall. Lonnie ends up in the electric chair, and is fried "live" on prime-time TV as part of a jazzy production number! "Fizzles with pixilated laughter."—Time. "I don't often burst into gales of laughter in the theatre; here, I found myself rocking with guffaws."—New York Mag. "Vastly entertaining."—Newark Star-Ledger.

(Royalty, $50-$40.)

SORROWS OF STEPHEN
(ADVANCED GROUPS—COMEDY)

By PETER PARNELL

4 men, 5 women—Unit set

Stephen Hurt is a headstrong, impetuous young man—an irrepressible romantic—he's unable not to be in love. One of his models is Goethe's tragic hero, Werther, but as a contemporary New Yorker, he's adaptable. The end of an apparently undying love is followed by the birth of a grand new passion. And as he believes there's a literary precedent for all romantic possibilities justifying his choices—so with enthusiasm bordering on fickleness, he turns from Tolstoy, to Stendhal or Balzac. And Stephen's never discouraged—he can withstand rivers of rejection. (From the N.Y. Times.) And so his affairs—real and tentative—begin when his girl friend leaves him. He makes a romantic stab at a female cab driver, passes an assignation note to an unknown lady at the opera, flirts with an accessible waitress—and then has a tragic-with-comic-overtones, wild affair with his best friend's fiancée. "Breezy and buoyant. A real romantic comedy, sophisticated and sentimental, with an ageless attitude toward the power of positive love."—N.Y. Times.

(Royalty, $50-$40.)

Other Publications for Your Interest

THE OCTETTE BRIDGE CLUB
(LITTLE THEATRE—COMIC DRAMA)
By P.J. BARRY

1 man, 8 women—Interior

There are no less than *eight wonderful roles for women* in this delightful sentimental comedy about American life in the 30's and 40's. On alternate Friday evenings, eight sisters meet to play bridge, gossip and generally entertain themselves. They are a group portrait right out of Norman Rockwell America. The first act takes place in 1934; the second act, ten years later, during a Hallowe'en costume/bridge party. Each sister acts out her character, climaxing with the youngest sister's hilarious belly dance as Salome. She, whom we have perceived in the first act as being somewhat emotionally distraught, has just gotten out of a sanitarium, and has realized that she must cut the bonds that have tied her to her smothering family and strike out on her own. This wonderful look at an American family in an era far more innocent and naive than our own was quite a standout at the Actors Theatre of Louisville Humana Festival of New American Plays. The play did not succeed with Broadway's jaded critics (which these days just may be a mark in its favor); but we truly believe it is a perfect play for Everybody Else; particularly, community theatres with hordes of good actresses clamoring for roles. "One of the most charming plays to come to the stage this season . . . a delightful, funny, moving glimpse of the sort of lives we are all familiar with—our own."—NY Daily News "Counterpunch". (#17056)

(Royalty, $60-$40.)

BIG MAGGIE
(LITTLE THEATRE—DRAMA)
By JOHN B. KEANE

5 men, 6 women—Exterior/Interior

We are very proud to be making available for U.S. production the most popular play by one of contemporary Ireland's most beloved playwrights. The title character is the domineering mother of four wayward, grown-up children, each determined to go his own way, as Youth will do—and each likely headed in the wrong direction. Maggie has been burdened with a bibulous, womanizing husband. Now that he has died, though, she is free to exercise some control over the lives of herself and her family, much to the consternation of her children. Wonderful character parts abound in this tightly-constructed audience-pleaser, none finer than the role of Maggie—a gem of a part for a middle-aged actress! "The feminist awareness that informs the play gives it an intriguing texture, as we watch it unfold against a colorfully detailed background of contemporary rural Ireland. It is at times like hearing Ibsen with an Irish brogue."—WWD. (#4637)

(Royalty, $50-$40.)

Other Publications for Your Interest

THE CURATE SHAKESPEARE AS YOU LIKE IT
(LITTLE THEATRE—COMEDY)
By DON NIGRO

4 men, 3 women—Bare stage

This extremely unusual and original piece is subtitled: "The record of one company's attempt to perform the play by William Shakespeare". When the very prolific Mr. Nigro was asked by a professional theatre company to adapt *As You Like It* so that it could be performed by a company of seven he, of course, came up with a completely original play about a rag-tag group of players comprised of only seven actors led by a dotty old curate who nonetheless must present Shakespeare's play; and the dramatic interest, as well as the comedy, is in their hilarious attempts to impersonate all of Shakespeare's multitude of characters. The play has had numerous productions nationwide, all of which have come about through word of mouth. We are very pleased to make this "underground comic classic" widely available to theatre groups who like their comedy wide open and theatrical. (#5742)

(Royalty, $50-$25.)

SEASCAPE WITH SHARKS AND DANCER
(LITTLE THEATRE—DRAMA)
By DON NIGRO

1 man, 1 woman—Interior

This is a fine new play by an author of great talent and promise. We are very glad to be introducing Mr. Nigro's work to a wide audience with *Seascape With Sharks and Dancer*, which comes directly from a sold-out, critically acclaimed production at the world-famous Oregon Shakespeare Festival. The play is set in a beach bungalow. The young man who lives there has pulled a lost young woman from the ocean. Soon, she finds herself trapped in his life and torn between her need to come to rest somewhere and her certainty that all human relationships turn eventually into nightmares. The struggle between his tolerant and gently ironic approach to life and her strategy of suspicion and attack becomes a kind of war about love and creation which neither can afford to lose. In other words, this is quite an offbeat, wonderful love story. We would like to point out that the play also contains a wealth of excellent **monologue** and **scene material.** (#21060)

(Royalty, $50-$35.)

Other Publications for Your Interest

CAT'S PAW
(LITTLE THEATRE—DRAMA)
By WILLIAM MASTROSIMONE

2 men, 2 women—Interior

This is a gripping drama about terrorism; but it does not come at the subject in a way you'd expect. When we think of "the terrorist", we generally think of a wild-eyed religious or political fanatic. What if, posits the acclaimed author of *The Woolgatherer*, *Extremities*, *Shivaree* and *Nanawatai*, a terrorist came along who was brilliant, who was articulate and who was *right*? Victor is the head of a terrorist group which is responsible for a bomb attack against the White House in which 27 people have been killed. He has arranged to have a television news reporter led to his lair, there to tell the world why he has done what he has done. Victor's obsession is the destruction of the world's water supply, and with it the final destruction of the human race, by pollution. When the reporter asks him if he feels any guilt about the death of the 27 innocent people, he replies that hundreds of innocent people are dying every hour because of what mankind is doing to its water supply—and do the people responsible feel guilt for this? This cat-and-mouse game between the young woman reporter and Victor gets more and more tense, leading to a shocking and violent conclusion. A standing-room-only hit at Seattle Repertory Theatre and later at San Diego's Old Globe. "An agonizingly suspenseful thriller."—San Diego Tribune. "A grabber."—Seattle Times. "Timely, thought-provoking and definitely worth seeing."—San Diego Reader. "Entertaining, informative, thoughtful and scary."—The Weekly (Seattle). (#5056)

(Slightly Restricted. Royalty, $50–$35.)

SHIVAREE
(LITTLE THEATRE—COMIC DRAMA)
By WILLIAM MASTROSIMONE

2 men, 3 women—Combination interior

We are delighted to publish this lesser-known but wonderful play by the acclaimed author of *Extremities* and *The Woolgatherer*. The story concerns a young hemophiliac youth named Chandler who has been kept, of necessity, by his cab driver mother in a very sheltered sort of existence. Chandler is desperate for contact with the world. He is also highly intelligent; but is supremely naive about the ways of the world. He pays a neighbor to bring him a girl; but he can't go through with his plans to have sex with her. He just doesn't know what to do about his craving for love—until he meets Shivaree. She is another neighbor who supports herself by being an itinerant belly-dancer. She is a True Original, and before too long the delightful Shivaree and the innocent Chandler are in love, much to the consternation of Chandler's mother, who forbids Chandler to ever see Shivaree again, throwing Shivaree out of Chandler's room. Chandler, undaunted, climbs out the fire escape—his first venture outside his hermetic world—going after his love. Fans of Mr. Mastrosimone's other plays will recognize the true-ness of the characterizations and the poignancy and humor of typical Mastrosimone dialogue in this wonderful play. (#21689)

(Royalty, $50–$35.)